D1601559

# KOREAN
# REUNIFICATION

# KOREAN REUNIFICATION

## ALTERNATIVE PATHWAYS

*Edited by* Michael Haas

PRAEGER

New York
Westport, Connecticut
London

**Library of Congress Cataloging-in-Publication Data**

Korean reunification: Alternative Pathways / [complied by] Michael
 Haas.
    p. cm.
  Rev. papers originally presented at various conferences.
  Bibliography: p.
  Includes index.
  ISBN 0–275–93148–X (alk. paper)
  1. Korean reunification question (1945–  )  I. Haas, Michael.
DS917.25.K685   1989
951.9′04—dc19          88–25189

Library of Congress Catalog Card Number: 88–25189
ISBN: 0–275–93148–X

First published in 1989

Praeger Publishers, One Madison Avenue, New York, NY   10010
A division of Greenwood Press, Inc.

Printed in the United States of America

The paper used in this book complies with the
Permanent Paper Standard issued by the National
Information Standards Organization (Z39.48–1984).

10   9   8   7   6   5   4   3   2   1

For the "Hawaii/Korea Mafia"

# Contents

Tables and Figures  ix

Abbreviations  xi

Preface  xiii

Introduction  xvii

1 The Historical Approach to Korean Reunification
  *Michael Haas*  1

2 The Neutralization Approach to Korean
 Reunification
  *Johan Galtung*  13

3 The Functionalist Approach to Korean Reunification
  *Michael Haas*  35

4 The Nonviolence Approach to Korean Reunification
  *Glenn D. Paige*  53

5 The Mediation Approach to Korean Reunification
  *Theodore L. Becker*  69

6 The Negotiation Approach to Korean Reunification
  *Oran R. Young*  91

7 The Political Feasibility Approach to Korean
 Reunification
  *Dae-Sook Suh*  117

Appendix A   Ten-Point Proposal for a Democratic
             Republic of Koryo
             *Kim Il Sung*                                    131

Appendix B   Proposal of 20 Pilot Projects to Facilitate
             National Reconciliation and Democratic
             Reunification
             *Republic of Korea*                             133

Select Bibliography                                          135

Index                                                        143

About the Contributors                                      151

# Tables and Figures

**TABLES**

| I.1 | Solutions to Korean Reunification | xix |
|-----|-----------------------------------|-----|
| 2.1 | Capitalism and Socialism as Economic Formations | 18 |
| 2.2 | Exchange Possibilities between Capitalist and Socialist Economies | 21 |
| 2.3 | Exchange Partners between Capitalist and Socialist Economies | 24 |
| 2.4 | Partners in Capitalist and Socialist Systems of Hegemony | 26 |
| 3.1 | Arenas for International Interaction | 41 |
| 3.2 | Proposals for Economic Cooperation, 1984 | 46 |
| 4.1 | Aging of Divided Korean Family Members | 59 |

**FIGURES**

| 4.1 | Nonviolent Combinatorial Creativity in Korea | 58 |
|-----|----------------------------------------------|----|
| 5.1 | Problem-Solving and Third Party Intervention | 82 |
| 6.1 | Negotiation Payoff Space | 95 |

# *Abbreviations*

| | |
|---|---|
| ASEAN | Association of South East Asian Nations |
| ASPAC | Asian and Pacific Council |
| COMECON | Council for Mutual Economic Assistance |
| DCRK | Democratic Confederal Republic of Koryo |
| DMZ | demilitarized zone |
| DPRK | Democratic People's Republic of Korea |
| ECDC | economic cooperation among developing countries |
| EEC | European Economic Community |
| ETMs | electronic town meetings |
| IOC | International Olympic Committee |
| IPU | Interparliamentary Union |
| MAC | Military Armistice Commission |
| NIEO | New International Economic Order |
| OPEC | Organization of Petroleum Exporting Countries |
| PRC | People's Republic of China |
| ROK | Republic of Korea |
| TPICR | third party international conflict resolution |
| UNC | United Nations Command |
| UNCTAD | United Nations Conference on Trade and Development |
| UNCURK | United Nations Commission for Unification and Rehabilitation of Korea |

# Preface

During my first trip to Korea, in mid-1971, I was on an assignment from the United Nations Institute for Training and Research to determine the relationship, if any, that could be developed between the UN system and the Asian and Pacific Council (ASPAC). Kim Kwang-Woong, the first student whose dissertation committee I chaired, remained in Hawaii to put finishing touches on his approved dissertation draft, but he arranged to have a member of his family provide entertainment and transportation during my stay in Seoul. In the course of my interviews I quickly learned that ASPAC was an extension of the foreign policy of the Republic of Korea, which was engaged in a "cold war" rhetoric regarding not just the Democratic People's Republic of Korea to the North but all countries with socialist economic systems allied with either China or the Soviet Union. By the end of the year the People's Republic of China was a member of the United Nations, President Park Chung-Hee continued in office as President of South Korea by means of a military coup, and support for ASPAC was considerably on the wane.

When I returned to Hawaii, I was greeted by Ahn Chung-Si and Kim Kook-Chin, two more students from Korea. In those days there were more graduate students from Korea in our Department than from any other country in Asia; they gathered for lunch beneath the banyan trees alongside the social science building, and in effect taught each other. I ended up chairing more dissertation committees for the Korean students than anyone else in the Department, and I served as a member of some of the other committees of the Korean students.

During my next visit, in late 1977, I was the guest of the Ministry of Foreign Affairs, Republic of Korea, still headed by President Park. Several of my students from the University of Hawaii had graduated and returned to Korea; one was a scholar at the Foreign Ministry's Institute of Foreign Affairs and National Security. A number of scholars were being invited by the Institute to present new perspectives on Asian international politics, and I was among the first. I was informed that my talk was viewed as an effort to shift "cold war" thinking within the Foreign Ministry toward other options, such as economic and technical cooperation. The discourse of the Republic of Korea was perceived as out of step with the rest of Asia and the world, in other words, and my role was to provide an alternative discourse which, if adopted, would better serve the interests of the Korean people. My talk, the thesis about the "Asian Way to Peace" was warmly received by some in the Ministry, and understandably resisted by others who were reluctant to ignore the ever-present threat that they perceived from the North. In time the transformation in thinking to a Korean economic cooperation offensive did take place, a fact that I observed when I returned the following year on a second sabbatical tour of Asian countries.

It was during the trips in 1977 and 1978 that I first heard the expression "Hawaii mafia" applied to the various Ph.D. graduates from the Department of Political Science, University of Hawaii. I was informed that we had graduated more Korean Ph.D.'s than any other graduate program in political science in the United States. Korean scholars with degrees from other universities noted that recent graduates from our Department were articulate, cohesive, energetic, highly research-oriented, and extremely well-trained, methodologically and theoretically. As the graduate adviser to so many of these students, I found myself playing the role of "godfather." I am therefore dedicating this book to the so-called "Hawaii mafia," as they alone have made it possible.

In 1980, a coup had brought General Chun Doo-Hwan to power in South Korea. At least one of his advisers was a former graduate student in the Department of Political Science, University of Hawaii at Manoa. A new foreign policy, formally adopting functionalist perspectives as the basis for dealing with North Korea, was announced. The Ministry of National Unification, accordingly, invited me to present a paper on the functionalist approach to reunification in 1982, though the paper was read at the very end of an exhaustive conference of papers. In 1987, I was asked to update my paper at a conference sponsored by the Korean Association of International Relations.

Other scholars around the world doubtless have similar stories to tell. Indeed, when my former colleague Ted Becker announced that he was about to embark on a trip to a conference in Korea, I realized that at least five persons at the University of Hawaii at Manoa had gone to Korea to share their ideas on Korean reunification over the past several years but had never exchanged their papers with one another. In an effort to share resources, I organized a symposium in early 1988, which turned out to be lively and intense. My suggestion to integrate the papers into a single volume was readily accepted by all. I then contacted Oran Young, whose paper at the 1982 conference in Korea had been unusually outstanding, and Dan Eades of Praeger Publications responded to my inquiry by providing a contract to publish the collection of essays.

Accordingly, some acknowledgments must be given, as earlier versions of the papers were considered publishable in a variety of forms. We are grateful for the opportunity to reprint Oran R. Young's "Korean Reunification: Alternative Theoretical Perspectives" from *Korea & World Affairs*, volume 7, number 1 (pp. 57–80), a revision of a paper originally presented at the Second International Symposium on Korean Reunification at Seoul during October 10–12, 1982. My own paper at this conference, subsequently revised, was published in the *Journal of Peace Research*, volume 21, number 1 (pp. 47–60), then substantially revised for the Korean Association of International Relations' Korean Reunification Revisited conference at Seoul during August 19–22, 1987, where my colleague Dae-Sook Suh also presented a paper. We are indebted to the Korean Association of International Relations for allowing us to publish two essays from volume 27, number 1, of *The Korean Journal of International Relations*—Michael Haas, "Functionalist Models for Korean Reunification" (pp. 139–62) and Dae-Sook Suh, "Domestic Environment for Korean Reunification" (pp. 193–206), and I wish to thank the Peace Research Institute of Oslo for permission to reproduce portions of the original article in the *Journal of Peace Research*. Finally, we wish to give acknowledgment to Sanchodo publishing company in Tokyo for allowing us to present the full text of Glenn D. Paige's "Nonviolent Global Transformation and Peaceful Korean Reunification," which was presented to the International Symposium on the Reunification of Korea and Peace in Asia, sponsored by the Asian-Pacific Peace Policy Institute, Yokohama, July 6–8, 1985. An abridged version, translated into Japanese, appeared on pages 92–103 in a volume of proceedings entitled *Chosen Toitsu to Ajia no heiwa* (Reunification of Korea and Peace in Asia).

Although the essays of Ted Becker and Johan Galtung appear for the first time in this volume, they have earlier origins. The Becker paper was delivered to the International Conference on Divided Nations: Reality and Vision, held at Seoul during October 28–31, 1987. The Galtung paper is a conjunction of three: a paper at the conference on Peace and Unification on the Korean Peninsula in a New International Order, Seoul, September 9–13, 1975; a European University Seminar on the Korean Question, Oslo, September 13–14, 1980; and a talk given to the Association of Korean Students, University of Hawaii, on January 10, 1986.

We are pleased to have this opportunity to share our thoughts on Korean reunification with a wider audience. It is our hope that the spirit of optimism, tempered with a goodly dose of realism, may serve in some humble way to bring Korea together.

*Michael Haas*
*Honolulu*

# Introduction

To the casual observer, the Korean War of 1950–53 ended in an armistice that remains unbroken over the past 35 years. U.S. troops remain, but they are stationed all over the world in countries that appear to be in no immediate danger of attack. For Koreans, the reality of the division between the Republic of Korea in the South and the Democratic People's Republic of Korea in the North is quite different. Both governments expect the other to attack any day, and they remain armed, with military cliques holding dominant positions in domestic politics. The moves of the other side are interpreted almost entirely as maneuvers intended to gain military and propaganda advantage in a continuing "cold war." Several million Koreans, however, have family members on the other side of the demilitarized zone between the two countries whom they have not seen for 35 or so years. The yearning for reunification is extremely strong among all Koreans. The two governments, therefore, must pay lip service to the goal of reunification. But since reunification might mean that one of the two regimes would have to capitulate the other, the continued division maintains in power two sets of military elites. An effort to reunify, even on paper if not in fact, would tear asunder the premise that the military on both sides of the peninsula are needed to safeguard the people from imminent attack, and civilian rule would result. Meanwhile, economic forces in both countries provide pressure to concentrate on civilian matters and to marginalize military considerations. The spectacular economic gains of the South have been associated with the rise of civilian capitalist elites and a middle class that find unprofitable and unseemly the system of military rule with its associated system of payoffs from business to governmental elites. Economic collapse in the North is viewed as a result of operating an economy in which ideological and military priorities have taken precedence over basic economic socialist principles; a more pragmatic approach, following the example of China and the Soviet Union, is viewed as preferable among the younger technocrats who desire to satisfy basic human needs for their people.

In 1981, the International Olympic Committee (IOC) decided to hold the Summer Olympics of 1988 in Seoul. As Korea is a divided country, IOC had in effect provided an opportunity to place Korean reunification on the agenda for serious discussion. As government leaders in the South viewed the decision as a form of international recognition that would bring enhanced credibility to its own views in its struggle with the North, Pyongyang had no alternative but to design a response. Old proposals were dusted off, and negotiations in due course were held between representatives of the two countries. The idea of a joint Korean team was proposed for the 1980 Olympics in Los Angeles, but the boycott by socialist countries saved the South from the need to decline the offer. As the Seoul Olympics drew nearer, the North proposed that Pyongyang serve as co-host for half of the games. IOC then sought to mediate between South and North to resolve the matter, fearing that the Games might be boycotted or disrupted if the North were not appeased. Discussions proceeded, but in November 1987, a bomb planted aboard a Korean Air flight exploded in midair, and negotiations involving North Korea ceased.

A strategist seeking to put in disarray the careful diplomatic efforts of the North could hardly have designed anything more effective than the bomb on the Korean Air flight. The South in due course announced that the bomb had been planted by an agent of the North, and one of the alleged saboteurs confessed after interrogation in Seoul. In view of the fact that the North was simultaneously conducting a peace offensive, two theories emerged. One theory is that hardliners in the North used the bomb to stop the pragmatists; if so, they succeeded. A second theory is that hardliners in the South trained the so-called saboteur so as to discredit the North as well as the more moderate elements in the Republic of Korea who had been working toward a detente between the two regimes; if this was the objective, it also worked. The only concrete evidence was the confession of someone who had been bribed by someone to engage in mischief. The result was yet another intermission in efforts at Korean reunification, which were leading to an easing of tensions on the peninsula.

This volume is written by scholars who have been concerned about Korean reunification and have suggestions to make along the lines of their expertise. All of the authors agree that discussions on Korean reunification should continue so that the conflict can be managed more peacefully in the years ahead.

**Table I.1**
**Solutions to Korean Reunification**

|  |  | Extent of Nongovernmental Contact | |
| --- | --- | --- | --- |
|  |  | High | Low |
| Extent of Inter-govern-mental Contact | High | federation | confederation |
| | Low | neutralization | detente |

What theory of international relations is appropriate for analyzing efforts to reunify Korea? One approach is to see the actions and inter-actions as chess moves motivated by desires to enhance national power. A second approach is to find fault on one side or the other, instances of prevarication or examples of negotiation in bad faith. Although these two methods of analysis may provide insights that can satisfy some onlookers, neither holds out any promise of resolving, containing, or freezing the conflict.

At least four approaches have been developed in regard to Korea in recent years (Table I.1). One is a *federal* solution, whereby two separate states would merge their foreign affairs, military defense, economic systems, and system of jurisprudence and judiciary, reserving some limited power in social matters to the separate regimes in North and South. This is an official position of the current plan of the Republic of Korea. A second approach is *confederation*, in which defense and foreign affairs would be handled by the central body but economic, legal, and social matters would be handled by ROK and DPRK as they wish. The North Korean plan is one of confederation of a state to be called Koryo. *Neutralization*, which entails the demilitarization of the peninsula, does not require a new political form but it cannot work unless there is considerable social and economic interaction between North and South, so a loose coordinating committee is assumed to be all that would be needed to ensure that it would be viable. (One of the principal advocates of neutralization is Johan Galtung, whose proposal appears later in this volume.) A *detente* is a minimalist approach, whereby the two governments would reduce tensions and establish an uninterrupted political dialog so that reunion visits of divided families, economic exchange, and other limited social and cultural interactions could occur and grow without incident. Most observers of Korea, including the official plans of North and South, presuppose a detente. They differ on steps required to develop a detente.

Several academic approaches have been suggested for managing the inter-Korean conflict that might lead to a detente or toward higher level forms of cooperation, including neutralization, confederation, or eventual federation. One approach is known as *functionalism*, which stresses informal contacts coupled with negotiations. The development of a culture of *nonviolence* is a second approach. A third approach is to promote skills at *mediation*; a related strategy is to develop a program of *negotiation* through a gradual series of unilateral moves of de-escalation reciprocated gradually by the other side, leading up to a conference that can yield progress through prior confidence-building measures. One cannot leave out the *political feasibility* approach, as any proposed solution for problems in Korea must take into account realities of domestic politics in both countries.

This volume is organized to review all of these approaches. In Chapter 1, Michael Haas provides a condensed summary of the history of reunification plans and negotiations. In Chapter 2, Johan Galtung argues the case for a neutralized Korea on the basis of theories of the conditions for associative behavior. In Chapter 3, Michael Haas provides perspective on functionalist strategies, that is, the approach in which the agenda between the two countries would be divided into subtopics in the hope that progress toward a detente and beyond can be achieved in some functional areas even when there are deadlocks in other arenas for cooperative activities. Glenn D. Paige, in Chapter 4, develops the notion of the need for a nonviolent culture; his plea is for the two regimes to cultivate the view, based on the devastation of the Korean War, that violence between Koreans is intolerable. In Chapter 5, Theodore L. Becker applies the theory and practice of mediation at the subnational level to the inter-Korean conflict. Oran R. Young, in Chapter 6, demonstrates that bargaining and negotiation could yield results useful to both Koreas; such efforts could begin with unilateral, reciprocated steps from the South, paralleled by similar moves from the North, leading to more tangible progress at the bargaining table. In Chapter 7, Dae-Sook Suh provides a healthy dose of realism as an antidote to the idealism of the other chapters; he notes that domestic political realities constrain decisionmakers to embark on a venturesome path. Appendixes contain texts of the major proposals that have been the primary agenda for discussions on reunification in the 1980s.

It is the view of all that the topic of Korean reunification will remain alive for some time. Progress toward an end to the Korean "cold war" will require attention to the theoretical approaches outlined herein.

# KOREAN REUNIFICATION

# 1     *The Historical Approach to Korean Reunification*
### Michael Haas

## KOREAN UNIFICATION AND INTERNATIONAL RELATIONS THEORY

Korea is a corner of the contemporary world with a protracted conflict dating back some 40 years. The division of the peninsula into North and South, two regimes that differ in terms of economic and political systems, has been less peaceful than the partition of Germany but more so in recent years than the division of Palestine. While a detente has been achieved between the two Germanies, and Palestine is beset with almost continual paramilitary forays, efforts at reunification of the two Koreas continue to be discussed.

In 1981, the International Olympic Committee (IOC) agreed to accept Seoul's invitation to host the Summer Olympics in 1988. The rest of the world, which had tried to stay out of the North-South conflict in Korea, was destined to become more aware of the nature of the struggle between the two regimes right up to the opening ceremony in September 1988. It has therefore become increasingly clear that something odd has been taking place on the peninsula over the years: responding to pressures from public opinion, plans for reunification have been announced back and forth over the last four decades, some of the positions have changed dramatically, yet the two governments remain as far apart as ever. How could this be so?

Traditionally, international relations theory focuses on power maximization or on idealistic elements, such as human rights, to find guides to policy. The Korea case, however, does not fit so neatly into such a framework. The aim of this chapter is to discuss negotiations among the two Koreas to achieve unification. In the process it will become clear that the two Koreas have flip-flopped positions yet remained intransigent over the years.

## NEGOTIATIONS FOR KOREAN UNIFICATION

Presently, there are two regimes on the Korean peninsula. The Democratic People's Republic of Korea (DPRK) is in control of the North, with a capital at Pyongyang. The Republic of Korea (ROK), with a capital city in Seoul, has jurisdiction over the South. The two Koreas are divided by a neutral body of land, known as the demilitarized zone (DMZ).

Plans for Korean reunification have been developed since the peninsula was first divided after World War II under terms of the Moscow Conference on December 27, 1945, which resulted in the USA-USSR Joint Commission. The latter body was established after a two-power preparatory meeting at Seoul in early 1946. But the Commission proved to be a prop through which the Soviet Union and the United States set the stage for an extension of the cold war to Asia. In 1947, while the Soviet Union addressed the United Nations calling for a removal of all foreign forces from Korea, the United States asked for a peace conference to resolve differences regarding Korea. Both sides, thus, rejected each other's proposals due to differing agendas. The United States, believing that there was no alternative to the division of Korea, persuaded the United Nations in 1948 to establish a commission on Korea—later retitled the UN Commission for Unification and Rehabilitation of Korea (UNCURK)—to keep a forum for possible negotiations alive. Soviet troops withdrew, but U.S. armed forces remained. One of the earliest plans for a confederation of Korea was articulated in a speech by DPRK's Kim Il Sung on June 2, 1948. During the following year the North applied for separate admission to the United Nations and organized the Democratic Front for the Reunification of the Fatherland, the latter consisting of political parties and social organizations on both sides of the 38th parallel that initially divided the two Koreas.

But within two years, on June 27, 1950, the Korean War broke out. On July 14, 1950, control over the armed forces of South Korea passed to what was called the United Nations Command (UNC), headed by U.S. General Douglas MacArthur. The United States military remained in control of the ROK army even after the armistice that ended the war in 1953. The United States signed an Armistice Agreement at Panmunjom on behalf of the South on July 27, 1953, but South Korean President Syngman Rhee refused to enter into the agreement. The Military Armistice Commission (MAC), set up by the agreement to hear complaints about violations of the armistice across the demilitarized zone (DMZ) established to separate the two Koreas, is charged with the responsibility of transforming the armistice into a peace accord, but its actual agenda has consisted of the former rather than the latter. Since no ROK President has signed the Armistice Agreement, ROK has only had an observer role at subsequent Panmunjom meetings of the MAC.

Seoul in effect surrendered its military sovereignty to the United States in 1950. South Korea now has an estimated 600 to 700 nuclear warheads on its soil at Kunsan Air Base entirely under U.S. control without any equivalent weapons in the North (Henderson, 1987, p. 38). As Seoul has continued to refuse to sign the Korean Armistice, Pyongyang had no alternative but to perceive South Korea as a satrapy of the United States. Although the United States is in command of the ROK army, it does not have chain-of-command control; the army of the Republic of Korea alone handles assignments, promotions, courts-martial, and the like. Hence, ROK troop movements associated with the coups of May 16, 1961, and December 12, 1979, were attributed in some quarters to the U.S. military presence, though the ROK army did not consult with or even notify UNC of its actions.

Despite the ambiguities in the status of the Republic of Korea, DPRK President Kim Il Sung proposed a nonaggression treaty on March 7, 1955, and announced on August 14, 1960, that his confederal plan of 1948 was still open for discussion. Harking back to its post-armistice proposal of August 5, 1953, North Korea indicated that some preliminary steps to a confederation might be necessary, including an economic commission of business circles in North and South, cultural exchanges, troop reductions, and a conference of representatives of governments, political parties, social organizations, and distinguished persons from the peninsula. The Republic of Korea rejected the proposal in 1953 and 1960 because it seemed to entail recognition of the two Koreas as sovereign equals, and the South was not ready to deal with the North on any basis.

The situation changed dramatically on July 25, 1969, when the Nixon Doctrine insisted that U.S. military involvement in world affairs would be only used to supplement contributions of friendly nations defending their own sovereignty where there were ongoing hostilities. Simultaneously, Nixon took steps to reach Sino-American and Soviet-American detentes. The first substantial application of the Nixon Doctrine was in Korea, where 20,000 U.S. troops were withdrawn in the fall of 1970. The Second U.S. Army pulled out in November, Camp Kaiser was transferred to the control of the ROK army, and the Seventh U.S. Army departed during the following March. Primary responsibility for the defense of South Korea was assumed to revert to the ROK armed forces, though the latter remained technically under the control of the UN Command. On July 4, 1971, Major General Felix Rogers, outgoing Chief Delegate representing the UNC, used the occasion of a final interview with Associated Press to express the hope that the Koreas would talk to each other to come to yet another detente in the world. Five days later a delegate from the People's Republic of China, absent for the past five years at Panmunjom, returned to be ready for the next meeting of the UNC. On July 15, Nixon announced that he would visit Beijing during February 1972.

Peace initiatives of North Korea, reiterated on April 13, 1971, in the form of a proposal by the DPRK Supreme People's Assembly, were then taken more seriously by the Seoul government, which was also reacting to the sizable vote cast for opposition leader Kim Dae Jung in the race for president. On August 12, 1971, the President of the South Korean Red Cross Society proposed a conference between the Red Cross Societies of North and South to discuss measures for reunion visits of families divided by the DMZ. Following acceptance of this proposal by the North two days later, the two societies met in working-level sessions on August 20, 1971, at Panmunjom, followed by a more lengthy session one month later on September 20. On January 1, 1972, DPRK President Kim proposed a formal North-South peace treaty, though the South failed to make a detailed response. In June 1972, U.S. Secretary of State William Rogers referred for the first time to the official name of North Korea as "Democratic People's Republic of Korea," and UN Secretary-General Kurt Waldheim received delegates from Pyongyang during a visit to Vienna in an effort to accelerate secret diplomacy regarding a possible detente between the two Koreas. Red Cross talks continued on a working-level basis until June 6, 1972, when an agenda was agreed upon for preliminary meetings.

Through the preliminary meetings, held later in June 1972, ground-work was laid for the North-South Joint Communique of July 4, 1972, simultaneously issued in Pyongyang and Seoul. The Joint Communique set forth common principles for direct intergovernmental negotiations through a North-South Coordinating Committee. One of the principles was to achieve unification without the interference of or reliance on outside forces, but ROK President Park Chung Hee clarified his understanding of the statement on the same day to mean that UN (and thus U.S.) forces were not considered to be "external," a repudiation that included by July 17 a promise that the South would achieve unification by means of "victory" over the North. Nonetheless, despite protests from President Kim over these seeming perfidies reported on September 19, formal bilateral Red Cross meetings began during the last half of 1972—at Pyongyang on August 30, then at Seoul on September 13.

During the third formal Red Cross meeting, held at Pyongyang on October 24–26, 1972, the South sought acceptance of a procedure for locating divided families, while the North insisted that anti-Communist propaganda should cease. Although a North Korean official shocked the South by referring to Kim Il Sung as the "beloved leader" of all Korean people during a speech at Seoul during September 1972, and President Park urged more anti-Communist education during an address the following month, both sides agreed to stop anti-North and anti-South propaganda on November 3, an agreement put into effect by November 11. But on October 30 the North announced a draft of a new constitution as a step toward reunification, stipulating that the unified capital was to be at Pyongyang (rather than Seoul). There was still no progress on reunion of divided families or any other issues, and by June 10, 1973, North Korean propaganda resumed.

By the seventh conference, held on July 12, 1973, the deadlock was clearly unbridgeable. When South Korean opposition leader Kim Dae Jung was kidnapped from a hotel in Tokyo by operatives of the Korean Central Intelligence Agency on August 8, 1973, a storm of protest emerged in Japan as well as in the North. By August 28, Pyongyang demanded that the South provide negotiators that Pyongyang would certify as true representatives of the people, thereby making any further dialog impossible.

While Red Cross meetings were taking place, the North-South Coordinating Committee met at Seoul during November 30 and December 1, 1972, then at Pyongyang on March 15, 1973, and at Seoul on June 12–14, 1973. The South proposed to set up three subcommittees (Cultural, Economic, Foreign Affairs), then two (Military, Political) as progress was achieved in the first three. The North insisted on setting up all five at once and put forward specific proposals relating to mutual troop reductions and the signing of a peace treaty. While the North did not demand a withdrawal of U.S. troops at the first Coordinating Committee meeting, this demand was advanced at the second meeting, doubtless because it appeared that the initial bargaining positions were so far apart that the conferences had already degenerated into occasions for propaganda and posturing. Both sides seemed prepared to jump to conclusions impugning each other's intentions without a more cautious and careful diplomacy. The logic announced by the South was to build up trust through less politicized areas of cooperation, while the North indicated that a concrete symbol of nonaggressive intentions should be signed as an immediate indication of mutual trust so that military and political tensions would not cloud efforts at progress on cultural exchange and economic cooperation.

But after July 12, 1973, the diplomacy ceased. Over 22 months there had been 58 conferences in which 2,337 members of the press and 1,084 negotiators were involved; 210 news reports and 315 officials crossed the DMZ (Chung, 1980: 155). A new North-South communications "hot line" was the only tangible result.

Following the entry of the People's Republic of China into the United Nations in October 1971, DPRK had been considering joining various international organizations as well. On April 23, 1973, the UN Conference on Trade and Development (UNCTAD) admitted North Korea. The Interparliamentary Union (IPU) followed suit, and the World Health Organization welcomed Pyongyang on May 17. Australia and Scandinavian countries exchanged diplomats with Pyongyang during this period. On June 23, 1973, the South switched its view and argued that there should be two Korean seats in the United Nations rather than the one seat which the North insisted was the inevitable concomitant of the South's acceptance of U.S. military dominance. Nonetheless, the North once again called for increased contact in cultural, diplomatic, economic, military, and political fields in response to the new position of the South of mid–1973. The South quickly denounced the North's simultaneous Great National Congress proposal and saw no basis for negotiation on the North's notion of a single Confederal Republic of Koryo as a member of the United Nations. By the end of 1973 UNCURK was removed at the insistence of the North.

Subsequently, the respective plans of the two regimes continued to diverge. The tendency to use the plans for propagandistic and strategic purposes has been assumed all along to mean that neither regime seriously intends to achieve unification but instead to say something to appease domestic pressure and world opinion while justifying continued military rule and restrictions on individual liberty on both sides of the DMZ.

On January 18, 1974, President Park proposed a nonaggression treaty based on the principles of noninterference and the continuation of the armistice. As the North has consistently wanted to conclude a full peace treaty, with the removal of the UN Command as a necessary consequence, Park's initiative was denounced in Pyongyang two days later. The DPRK People's Assembly then adopted a resolution on March 24, 1974, urging a bilateral peace treaty with the United States; subsequently, the North sought to deal with Washington over the heads of the regime in Seoul that was insisting upon continual U.S. military control in the South.

It was in this context that candidate Jimmy Carter suggested a withdrawal of U.S. forces from South Korea during the presidential campaign of 1976. Implementation of the idea was shelved due to considerable pressure brought to bear on President Carter as he took office in 1977. Instead, in 1978 a Combined Forces Command Agreement sought to rectify the anomaly of U.S. control over ROK armed forces by establishing an integrated staff and headquarters. But a U.S. general is still in charge, the agreement itself has never been made public, and the U.S. commander still expects to be informed of any South Korean troop movements. The second in command is a South Korean general, and the arrangement is usually touted as transitional to the removal of the UN Command. But no negotiations have ever resulted to carry the transition forward to an actual dismantling of the UNC.

With the World Table Tennis championships scheduled for April 1979, at Pyongyang, the DPRK proposed an inter-Korean sports meeting to discuss the possibility of a single Korean team. The South accepted the invitation, but after four rounds of discussions in February 1979, talks broke down. Although the South was excluded from the competition, the U.S. table tennis team participated in the tournament.

An opportunity for mediation was presented by UN Secretary-General Waldheim when he visited both Koreas in May 1979, but nothing resulted. President Carter, during his visit to Seoul on June 29-July 1, 1979, proposed talks involving the two Koreas and the United States. Both Koreas responded by insisting that the armistice must first become a peace treaty before ROK and DPRK would again have direct discussions. A few months later, using Hongkong as a trading intermediary, South Korea purchased several thousand tons of coal from North Korea.

President Park was assassinated on October 26, 1979, followed by a military coup. Opposition to the new regime, headed by General Chun Doo-Hwan, was particularly strong in the southwestern part of Korea, the home of Kim Dae-Jung, whose electoral success in mid–1971 had been nullified by Park's declaration of emergency and martial law by the end of 1971. President Chun soon called for a meeting with his opposite number, Kim Il Sung. Starting February 6, 1980, ten rounds of negotiations discussed a North-South Prime Ministers' meeting, again to no avail. On May 26–27, 1980, demonstrations outside a U.S. Information Agency facility at Kwangju led to the shooting of protesters by the army of the Republic of Korea in which approximately 200 civilians died. As the movement of troops to Kwangju was approved by a U.S. commander, anti-American sentiment within South Korea increased considerably after the Kwangju massacre. In order to respond to the sensitivity of South Koreans to the role of the United States, South Korea thereafter withdrew its Second Army (a training command), the Capital Division (which guards the ROK President), and the Special Warfare Forces (used at Kwangju) from the UN Command.

On October 10, 1980, the North issued a blueprint for a Democratic Confederal Republic of Korea, with a national congress, a unified army and foreign policy, and thus one Korea to be admitted to the United Nations. As a precondition, the North called for a peace treaty, a democratic regime in the South, and the removal of all U.S. military forces. After the new confederation, the North proposed economic cooperation and cultural exchange.

In January and June 1981, President Chun proposed an exchange of visits with President Kim. A more detailed proposal was then presented on January 22, 1982, in the form of an eventual Unified Democratic Republic of Korea. Among the elements in the 1982 plan are exchanges among ordinary citizens, a summit conference of heads of the two Koreas, recognition of two Koreas in the United Nations, and a referendum on a new constitution to reflect the will of the Korean people. Cross-recognition of DPRK by allies of the South, and vice versa for ROK by the North's allies, has also been a part of the plan; this is due to the fact that it was an element of the detente between East and West Germany in 1972, though it has nothing to do with unification per se.

The propagandistic elements of the two latest proposals, as usual, detract from some of the good points. For example, it is unrealistic for the South to expect the North to agree to a unitary system based on elections. The North surely cannot expect a unified army or foreign policy, though Pyongyang claims that it does not want to impose its economic system on the South. On the other hand, the South should not rule out eventual removal of U.S. troops, and the North will get nowhere appearing to dictate how the South is to select members for the unified confederal parliament. But these are matters for negotiation.

In 1981, as noted already, the Republic of Korea chalked up a considerable propaganda coup when the International Olympic Committee accepted Seoul as the site for the 1988 Summer Olympic Games. This permitted at least seven years for the North to determine a response, and the South stonewalled negotiations through the IOC until Pyongyang gave up and unsuccessfully tried to organize a boycott. Seoul was also chosen to host the 1986 Asian Games, and North Korean athletes were not allowed to participate, also due to the intransigence of the South.

In 1983, there were confusing signals on the peninsula. North Korea asked China to assist in establishing talks with the United States, then one day after this initiative came the Rangoon bombing that killed 17 South Koreans, including heads of government departments. As two North Korean army officers were later convicted of the crime, we are left with the inference that opinion in the DRPK government was sharply divided with regard to a North-South detente.

In January 1984, Pyongyang proposed a tripartite conference, with the two Koreas and the United States present, to sign a U.S-North Korean peace treaty and a North-South nonaggression pact, but both

South Korea and the United States rejected the proposal. Instead, inter-Korean talks resumed: In March there were three unsuccessful rounds of discussion on North Korea's proposal for a single Korean team to the 1984 Olympic Games at Los Angeles; in November the South accepted the North's offer to ship food to victims of a flood in the South, whereupon talks again ensued. Focusing on economic issues, government officials met at Panmunjom for the South-North Economic Meeting in 1984, then Red Cross talks took place at Seoul and Pyongyang through September 1985. A meeting of parliamentarians was also held in this period.

But in January 1986, DPRK broke off these conferences, insisting that a precondition was discussion of such issues as the largest annual military exercises in the world—those involving 200,000 U.S. and ROK troops, known as "Team Spirit." Although the North offered to cease its own military exercises in return, and even suspended its 1986 exercises, the South refused to discuss the idea, and in 1987 Team Spirit was conducted on a larger scale than ever before. Then in mid–1986 the North proposed talks between the top defense officials of DPRK and ROK, along with the U.S. commander of forces in Korea; Seoul declined, arguing for the first time that it wanted direct North-South talks instead. In November 1986, Kim Il Sung proposed that DPRK and ROK Deputy Prime Ministers meet, but the South imposed preconditions that amounted to a reopening of the economic talks, noting that in 1972 East and West Germany had already signed a series of agreements governing common rivers, irrigation, and water resources. South Korea also expressed concern about the possible military implications of the Kumgangsan Dam under construction in the North. In December 1986, and January 1987, the North again proposed both military and Deputy Prime Minister talks, but it presented a new idea—a Neutral Nations Supervisory Commission, to be composed of representatives from Czechoslovakia, Poland, Sweden, and Switzerland to observe the demilitarization of the DMZ. The South replied in January 1987, that resumption of Red Cross and economic meetings as well as a summit conference were preconditions to the meetings proposed by the North. By July 23, 1987, the North was announcing a unilateral cut of 100,000 in its armed forces for work on the Kwangbok sports complex (for Friendship Games in 1989) and other development projects and was calling for talks in Geneva to negotiate arms reduction along the lines of the Strategic Talks for Arms Reduction (START) between the Soviet Union and the United States. DPRK's proposal would have the three countries with troops in Korea negotiate together with a view to a gradual reduction in military personnel from the present ratio of about 600,000 in the South and 800,000 in the North, starting in 1988, until there remained 100,000 on both sides by 1992 or 1997. The North again proposed that all 40,000 U.S. troops be withdrawn, but by the end of 1987 Pyongyang conceded that a phased withdrawal would be acceptable. South Korea's response by early August was to reject any such talks that would include the United States; instead, talks between Foreign Ministers were proposed for the time of the opening of the UN General Assembly in September, either in New York or elsewhere. The logic of the South was a need for "confidence-building measures" to increase mutual trust before agreeing to discuss a drastic shift in the power structure on the peninsula; one such confidence-building measure would have been to agree to discussions with the North on the latter's terms, but the South was not prepared to do so. The North, which failed to receive positive responses on troop reduction proposals from the South in 1954, 1973, 1986, turned down the Foreign Minister's conference idea.

By the end of 1987 North Korea appeared eager to show good faith in regard to issues of reunification and detente. Invitations were issued to various journalists and scholars to visit Pyongyang. DPRK officials assumed a pragmatic stance in which they believed that an eventual Communist unification was "completely out of the question" (Harrison, 1987). While opposition ROK leader Kim Dae-Jung was arguing for a "Confederation of Korean Republics" in his unsuccessful campaign for the presidency, President Chun greeted the idea with scorn. The North indicated that it was willing to discuss any confederation proposal as the "final stage" of unification (Harrison, 1987: 37). China, moreover, began to urge the United States to urge reason on intransigent Seoul lest hardliners in the North prevail over pragmatists.

The rise of Li Gun-Mo, an economic technocrat, to the position of Prime Minister in the North during 1987 cautiously heralded a new era of pragmatism. The South, meanwhile, appeared headed for a more democratic system, as Seoul demonstrators in mid–1987 succeeded in getting the government to establish a system of direct election of the president. In early 1988, Roh Tae-Woo, with backing from the ruling party, defeated challengers Kim Dae-Jung, Kim Young-Sam, and others in a reasonably fair and free election for the presidency. Roh campaigned with a pledge to provide more democratization for South Korea, and he promised that he would negotiate an arrangement whereby ROK would assume full operational control of its own military forces.

## THE OLYMPIC GAMES OF 1988

But North and South continued to differ on the Olympic Games. Not surprisingly, North Korea was eager to play host to at least half of the 23 sports on the program of the Olympics. Although the decision to hold the Olympics in Seoul was made in 1981, negotiations by the International Olympic Committee (IOC) did not begin until 1984. Pyongyang understandably insisted that it be made co-host city, a gesture that would help to ease tensions with no cost to either side, unusual as it would be in the history of the Games. In response, IOC offered a paltry two and one-half events (archery, table tennis, and the beginning of 100-kilometer road cycling) plus a soccer preliminary. In subsequent rounds of talks North Korea lowered its request to eight games, giving up its demand to hold either the opening or closing ceremonies for the Games in Pyongyang and agreeing to participate in cultural events in Seoul. Then in July 1987, North Korea appeared to drop its demand to five and one-half events. IOC increased the number of possible events to be held in the North to four and one-quarter (adding men's road cycling, women's volleyball, and a soccer preliminary), leaving disagreement centering on soccer, where the North wanted the full event and a preliminary in some other event. But Seoul left to IOC the efforts to reach a formula that would enable the North to save face in what was the largest diplomatic success yet enjoyed by the South. During 1987 North Korea refused to enter various qualifying meets, claiming that it was automatically entitled to participate since it was to be a co-host, though both Koreas were represented in the Asian Track and Field competition at Singapore in July 1987. We were in suspense on the matter until the deadline in January 1988, for formal acceptances of IOC invitations to participate in the Olympic Games.

But in November 1987, Korean Air 858 exploded midair over Burma. Investigations revealed that there was a bomb planted by two unknown saboteurs, one of whom committed suicide immediately, the other flown to Seoul for questioning. In a confession announced on January 17, 1988, shortly after formal acceptances of IOC invitations had been received by IOC, the saboteur was reported to be under orders from DPRK. The inference was that North Korean hardliners were trying to do something that might discourage countries from participating in the Olympic Games at Seoul. But the act of air piracy also played into the hands of South Korean hardliners that desired both Roh's election and a halt to the detente slowly developing between North and South throughout 1987. The result of the incident was a blow to North Korean pragmatists, as IOC decided to cease negotiation with the North in the wake of the sabotaged flight. The United States placed DPRK on its list of "terrorist nations," thereby ending all informal contacts between the two countries. Japan then agreed to cease all trade contact with the North, but relented within a few months when President Roh's overtures to the North resulted in a meeting of parliamentarians from both Koreas, recessed during the period of the Games, to discuss a joint nonaggression pact and other matters. Thus, opportunities for a detente between the two Koreas were again missed, but some remarkable progress occurred over the years. The possibility of repetitions of the bombed Korean Air 858 in 1987 and the bomb that went off in Seoul at the beginning of the Asian Games in 1986 were clouds over the Seoul Olympics, which went forward with the largest participation in 12 years. After the Olympics the continuing desire for a detente will again capture the imagination of sincere Koreans throughout the peninsula.

## REFERENCES

Chung, Dae-Haw. (1980). *Toward a Pluralistic Security Community: The Relevance of the Integration Theory for Divided Nations with Special Emphasis on the Case of Korea.* Philadelphia: unpublished Ph.D. diss., University of Pennsylvania.

Harrison, Selig. (1987). "The 'Great Follower': Kim Il Sung Promotes a Chinese-Style Open-Door Policy," *Far Eastern Economic Review*, 138, (December 2): 36–38.

Henderson, Gregory. (1987). "Time to Change the US-South Korea Military Relationship," *Far Eastern Economic Review*, 138 (October 22): 40.

# 2 The Neutralization Approach to Korean Reunification

*Johan Galtung*

## A CASE FOR OPTIMISM: THE T + 40 PRINCIPLE

In recent years little has happened to promote a reunification process for Korea. Nevertheless, there are reasons to make a prediction: By the year 2000 there will be some kind of reunification of that nation, so badly treated by history. In saying so it is assumed that the forces pushing the Korean nation together are by and large greater than the forces pulling the two countries, as they are defined today, apart. And these forces are not only found in the obvious superpower interests in addition to the interests of Japan and China: Korea is the only country in the world having the four biggest powers in the world of today as neighbors. (For the U.S. troops, stationed in close juxtaposition to the demilitarized zone between the two Koreas, maintenance of the status quo is part of the anti-Communist crusade.) Forces are also found inside the two Koreas as vested interests in the leaderships and differences between the two systems. In addition, one factor should not be underestimated: Many people have become accustomed to the situation and have become innovative in finding reasons why nothing will, or even should, happen; the badly needed imagination for a process of unification is a very scarce commodity. A solid propaganda war on both sides intensifies all of this.

Nevertheless, the prediction stands because of one significant factor—*the change of generations*. It took Germany 30 years, 1945–75, to produce a new generation able to look at the Nazi horrors and crimes with fresh eyes, launching Germany as a nation with at least to some extent a new identity. And it then took ten more years to initiate a process reunifying the nation (not the states). Correspondingly, it took Spain about 40 years after the Civil War of 1936–39, after the death of Franco in 1975, to launch the country on a democratic path, unifying people who when they were younger would have been bitterly opposed to each other to the point of settling accounts by killing each other. And it took China almost 40 years to initiate a process bringing the nation (again, not necessarily the states) together after the double trauma of a revolutionary process and the division of the country. So maybe it will take 40 years also for the two Koreas to produce a new generation after the trauma, the terrible war of 1950–53, including the passing away of the leader in the North. That would bring us into the early 1990s, leaving a sufficient number of years for a reasonable process to be completed by the year 2000.

I shall refer to this principle as the $T+40$ (trauma + 40 years) factor—the time needed for the trauma-struck generation to retire, biologically or socially, and for a new generation, not directly hit by trauma, to emerge.

In this reunification process I do not think that there is much to learn from Germany, but very much to learn from Austria; after all, the two Germanies are not unified, whereas Austria became a unity again in 1955. Of course, the differences are important. Germany was divided in order not to be united again, as a punishment, even as a revenge, for the horrors of war, as a preventive measure to stifle a German state with its proven inclinations, three times in one century. Korea was divided not because it was an enemy but as a part of the Japanese empire, not taking into account the Korean people's own heroic fight against Japanese imperialism, headed by Marxists and Christians, by leaders who became president in North Korea and South Korea, respectively. The division was a superpower convenience, and a clear expression of Occidental racism ("Who are those Koreans, what kind of people are they, who do they think they are?").

A consensus seems now to be building, both inside and outside Germany, that the country will not be unified as a state, whereas the unification of the nation, in the sense of persons, goods/services, and ideas crossing the borders freely is considered a birthright of the German nation. It should be as easy to cross from Bayern to Thuringen as from Bayern to Tirol, and vice versa, as the saying goes. Such sentiments do not surround the Korean peninsula; in that sense the situation has more similarity with Austria. Moreover, in the Austrian case it was the United States that held up unification more than the Soviet Union—a point that might be of interest to take into account in any future negotiations.

So much for the process, what about the *goal*? A unitary Korean state might be a long-term goal but is hardly realistic, given the differences of the two systems in the short term. Much more realistic is the goal put forward by the North—the Democratic Confederal Republic of Koryo (DCRK). The formulation preserves diversity within unity. It is interesting to compare this formulation of the goal with the corresponding list of 20 small steps put forward by South Korea: in the first case, a goal without much indication of the process; in the second case, very small, highly concrete process steps without much indication of the goal. Relatively typical of socialist-capitalist discourse in general, or in broader terms typical of change-oriented versus status quo-oriented systems. And that begs the immediate question: Could the process steps and the goal formulations be combined, if the political atmosphere improves at T + 40?

Again, Austria might be interesting as an example. There was once an Austro-Hungarian Empire; many Hungarians speak excellent German, some Austrians speak Hungarian. Today, after highly traumatic events in the late 1940s, one country is socialist, one country is capitalist. The interchange of people, goods and services, and ideas across the frontier is considerable today, at T + 40. It is not obvious that it is so problematic. If the two Korean neighbors could obtain the Austria-Hungary level of interaction, it would already be a great step forward. But does that not mean that, strictly speaking, a confederation is unnecessary? In a sense, yes, if it had not been for the fact that Korea is one nation, whereas Austria and Hungary are two. Symbolic, even institutional, recognition of that circumstance has to be given.

How could a confederation of this type assert itself in the international system? The basic point in the negotiations, which would have to involve all four powers mentioned above, would be an exchange of *unification for neutrality*, the latter implying withdrawal of all foreign troops and at the same time the creation of credible, nonprovocative, defensive defense. There are at least five models in Europe, each with something interesting to offer for the case of Korea.

Thus, from Switzerland Korea can learn about defensive defense and armed neutrality in general, and more particularly about the positive significance of a small, neutral country in a power field (Switzerland also used to be surrounded by four major powers) as a place where big powers in conflict can meet, have conferences, summit meetings, and what not. A unified Korea should make this a major mission in world affairs, even creating out of Panmunjom a Korean Geneva. As an aside, the economic value of that kind of industry is considerable.

From Austria a unified Korea can learn not only about the process of unification by studying intensely the history of the negotiations that neutralized Austria, but also about what it means, concretely, to be an active trade partner with powers on all sides. Austria displays a more active neutrality than Switzerland, hence there may be different things to learn from Calvinist/Protestant and Catholic approaches.

From Yugoslavia Korea can learn much, as also from Switzerland, about how to construct federations of which there are positive and negative aspects. In addition, the Yugoslavs offer another model of defensive defense, also of considerable interest to a unified Korea, more based on paramilitary and nonmilitary resistance.

From Sweden a unified Korea could learn many of the same things as she can learn from Austria. Active diplomacy from a basis of non-alignment, nonprovocative defense, and peace initiatives are central to the Swedish model.

And from Finland a unified Korea can learn something about the importance of having good connections with the more closed societies in the world system, the socialist countries of various types. No doubt North Korea will retain many socialist features for a long time to come, as well as contacts with the big countries bordering on that part of Korea. On the other hand, all socialist countries are now undergoing basic changes, probably leading to a much higher level of international interaction.

Thus not only does the *process* seem relatively feasible, provided a minimum of political will is present, but the *goal* is also attractive, not only for Korea but also for the Asian region and thereby for the world as a whole. What a process of this kind would mean is simply the defusion of a major source of conflict that could one day escalate into a terrible war, threatening not only to Koreas, but all of Asia and the whole world. Thus, there is a common world interest in settling the situation and a need for UN auspices for any major conference toward that goal.

In the longer run, however, it may be argued that a unitary state would better correspond to the aspirations of the Korean people—whether that proposition is empirically valid or not. What seems to be the case is that it is difficult to conceive of a unitary state without a more unitary economic system. And here there are, of course, three possibilities: all of Korea capitalist, all of Korea socialist, or all of Korea social democrat. The latter means meeting in the middle, where reason is located, according to the social democrats.

Of course, this is for Koreans to decide, and to decide in a democratic manner. But one point might be of interest here: It is not obvious that a unitary system is more cohesive than a diverse system with a well-working symbiosis between the two parts. Moreover, from a world economic point of view, it might be better for the country to practice the current Chinese philosophy of "one country, two systems" than to continue with the conventional European tradition of unity and unitary systems, which certainly have not stood the test of time. Interdependence is much stronger than convergence as a peace-building tie. After all, there is a contradiction between the two systems, which will be explored in the rest of this chapter. Any unity will be forced. A neutralized confederation is more subtle, more flexible. But the problem still remains: Can the two systems cooperate?

## IS PEACEFUL COOPERATION BETWEEN DIFFERENT SYSTEMS POSSIBLE?

Let us forget about Korea for a moment and imagine two countries, C and S, one a capitalist, the other a socialist country. We want to discuss the problems of interaction between them, not only in the form of exchange but also cooperation, meaning roughly that they do something together beyond the mere exchange of persons, goods, and ideas.[1] We shall start with the most basic properties of the two systems and then gradually fill in more details to make the picture somewhat more realistic.

What are the most basic properties? Liberalism and Marxism are broad, encompassing ideological systems; but, coming out of the late eighteenth- and nineteenth-century Europe, the shared focus is on economic aspects[2]—so dynamic at that time—and their social manifestations. Capitalism and socialism are above all socioeconomic formations, profoundly affecting production patterns, but also to some extent the patterns of consumption. In both systems production factors—land (ground, raw materials), labor (skilled, unskilled), capital (money, capital goods), research and management—are brought together, and there is processing into products, mainly taking place in factories, in the cities. Neither system is against industrialism.

But there are some important differences (Table 2.1). The differences are fundamental enough, but they are not located in the oft-mentioned distinction between private and collective ownership of the means of production. There is ample experience showing that the state as the owner of the means of production may practice entirely capitalist goals and methods.[3] The difference can be spelled out as follows. Under *capitalism* the ultimate measure of the success of an economic process is the accumulation of capital, leaving production for those who want and can pay for the products and to a "global reach"[4] when it comes to where to fetch factors and where to market products, investing capital into research so as to produce in an ever more efficient manner. Under *socialism*, essentially a family of related efforts to negate capitalism,[5] the production is, at least in the first phase, for the satisfaction of basic needs—meaning food, clothing, shelter, health, and education. There is much emphasis on using domestic factors and much less on

Table 2.1
Capitalism and Socialism as Economic Formations

|  | Capitalism | Socialism |
|---|---|---|
| Ownership of Means of Production | private | collective (state, communal) |
| Production for | demand, market | needs, basic need of most needy |
| Mobility of Factors and Products | unlimited, expansionist, trade | limited, national or local self-reliance, not autarchy |
| Production Methods | high productivity | lower productivity |

trade (particularly in the first phase of socialism) and on securing full employment, even on some measure of meaningful participation of everyone, at least rhetorically.

It may be objected that this is too sketchy and also too ideological. But that is exactly the purpose. These, it is claimed, are fundamental features of the "systems" that have grown up in Korea over the past 40 years. In much of the debate about peaceful coexistence the attention is so much on the political moves of the day that the basic underlying characteristics of the systems are easily forgotten. That both systems undergo modifications is obvious enough. Nevertheless, these features play a basic role politically in shaping the process of the highly uneasy relationship between capitalist and socialist states. The two are simply different systems and partly contradictory systems, though the ideal versions of both systems are simpler than the infinitely more complex empirical reality.

Differences between capitalism and socialism also show up in the indicators of economic activity. The capitalist system talks about economic growth and measures it in terms of processing and marketing, expressed in *gross national product* (per capita). The socialist system is more concerned with the level of *basic needs satisfaction*. The capitalist systems speak about *foreign trade* and see *increase in exports* as a major goal, whereas the socialist system is more concerned with how one can do without trade, in other words in *self-reliance*. The capitalist system focuses on how many units of output per capita and worker-hour input units, whereas the socialist system focuses on how many units of output one can get per unit of land or raw materials (which is also of interest to the capitalist system, of course). In general, the capitalist system seeks a decrease in the role of workers through higher labor productivity, while the socialist system seeks an increase in the role of labor through higher worker participation and, of course, full employment.

Let us now pursue these differences, economically and politically, to see what impact they have on efforts to achieve patterns of cooperation between the systems, with particular attention to Korea. We start with the economic sector.

## ECONOMIC RELATIONS BETWEEN THE TWO SYSTEMS

A basic assumption of the capitalist system is that other countries are willing to play the capitalist world game, that is, the game of trade, selling what they have in excess, and buying what they do not have— of factors and products alike. But a pure socialist system is not willing to play this game for many reasons. A socialist system wants to control its own land and natural resources and to use its capital and labor at home. It wants to develop its own research and management capability. It is skeptical if not totally against lasting import of capital and even of skilled technicians because such inputs tend to deform the local economic structure. There is equal skepticism of the import of manu-factured goods, except perhaps capital goods that may better facilitate the pursuit of a policy of self-reliance.

Hence, the point of departure is already far from positive when it comes to exchange, leaving alone cooperation between the two systems. What to the capitalist system is a natural thing, the normal way of operation, becomes to the socialist system economic aggression and something to protect oneself against. Experience proves the socialist thesis correct to a large extent: exploitation as a part of a general capitalist formation is a major characteristic of world trade. Socialism is above all adopted by countries in need of economic and political/military defense against economic and political/military invasion—Russia in 1917, Eastern European states after World War II, the North Korea and other Asian socialist countries, Cuba and Nicaragua—and other countries that have adopted somewhat similar patterns, such as Algeria.[6]

There are three kinds of answers to the problem of exchange: no interaction at all, interaction in noneconomic fields, or efforts to find some kind of economic interaction nonetheless. Leaving out the first and the second, because they are explored later and also because they often are even more problematic due to ideological differences, the question becomes: Is there some type of economic exchange that would be acceptable from both a capitalist and a socialist point of view?

We have mentioned one already—capital goods, usually in exchange for raw materials. This may take the form of technology, machine tools, factories, labor-saving devices (particularly in agriculture, transportation, and in the construction industries). In general, the exchange of capital goods plays into the hands of the more advanced capitalist countries if the latest technology is what is demanded, also because capitalists can afford to lose money on initial deals, hoping for more demand to follow. Generally, there will be capital export accompanying capital goods export, solidifying the control. But in Korea today the South imports primarily coal from the North. What about all of the other types of commodities?

In Table 2.2 we sort out the various types of commodities (in the broadest sense of that term) that capitalist and socialist countries may *export*, so each of the 49 cells gives one type of exchange. The typical case already mentioned, capital goods in exchange for raw materials, is marked A in Table 2.2.

In general, we would assume that capitalist countries, unless they are very big and very rich in natural resources, would be loathe to export raw materials. The same logic would apply to land and unskilled labor, unless these are dependent capitalist countries in the periphery of the system.[7] Dependent capitalist countries would probably export those products to their own center countries (vertical trade, as it is called), since that is what center countries will demand from them in exchange for consumer goods and capital goods. South Korea exports unskilled labor to the United States in the form of deep-sea fishing personnel and immigrants, but it also processes and finishes consumer goods for sale to the United States because its workforce, unskilled until recently, is accustomed to the low wages associated with periphery countries that export raw materials alone.

Correspondingly, we would imagine that the socialist countries would be loathe to export unskilled labor (against capital, the famous postal bank remittances), as that would be a complete capitulation to the world capitalist system. As Yugoslavia and Algeria export unskilled labor, the argument would run, it is because they are not really socialist. Socialist countries might want to export excess skilled labor,[8] capital, capital goods, and manufactured goods, however, and when they do not do so in the East-West setting in the West (or at least not much so), then it is not because they do not choose to, but because their products are not much in demand and/or the capitalist countries deliberately place them in the international division of labor as periphery countries, treating them much as they treat their colonial/neocolonial peripheries. In the case of North Korea, the view that its goods are

Table 2.2
Exchange Possibilities between Capitalist and Socialist Economies

| Capitalist \ Socialist | Land | Raw Materials | Unskilled Labor | Skilled Labor | Capital | Capital Goods | Products |
|---|---|---|---|---|---|---|---|
| Land | | | | | | | |
| Raw Materials | | C | | E | E | D,E | E |
| Unskilled Labor | | | | E | E | E | E |
| Skilled Labor | | B | B | | | | |
| Capital | | B | B | | | | |
| Capital Goods | | A,B | B | | | | |
| Products | | B | B | | | | E |

shoddy is spread by the United States, the quintessential center capitalist state, to ward off any serious discussion of possible trade, yet investors from Germany in recent years have made contracts with industrial plants in the North for the import of stockings and other clothing (Harrison, 1987).

Thus, in general, it is obvious that most of the exchange possibilities are located in the lower, left corner of Table 2.2. And this is also where that ingenious face-saving formula, the *joint venture*, is located. Instead of exchanging across borders, sending the factors to the West and letting the processing take place there, what is done is to move the factories to the factors and establish them as "joint ventures" inside the socialist countries. In practice, a joint venture involves the capitalist countries exporting skilled labor (technicians), capital, capital goods, and ultimately, also products (for example, cars, only that they do not cross borders) and the socialist counties contribute raw materials and unskilled labor and *markets* (B in Table 2.2). It is difficult to see that this "joint venture" differs from conventional vertical trade. The research spinoffs are still with the capitalist countries, which retain control over the dynamism of product development, and probably to a large extent are able to paralyze the enterprise, or at least lower its output qualitatively to a considerable extent, through withdrawal of essential capital and technology and technicians if there is a conflict. Hence, we shall not refer to this as cooperation but as trade in disguise, and vertical trade at that.

It is our basic contention that this kind of arrangement is contrary to the interests of socialist countries, that, broadly speaking, "joint ventures" imply that they have been cheated again by the by-and-large more clever elites in the capitalist countries. The ties established may have a certain binding function, but also a conflict-creating function, as postulated by Marx and Lenin. In all probability they will serve to make the socialist economies a dependent one. This does not mean poor or technologically unsophisticated economies, but economies incapable of setting their own goals and of experimenting with new means and modes of production the moment the turret is really open for the type of consumer goods produced in advanced capitalist countries, coveted and enjoyed by the new emerging elites in the socialist countries. And not only by them. Perhaps this is why North Korea has a healthy suspicion toward the joint ventures between the two countries proposed by South Korea among the 20 inter-Korean "pilot projects" (Appendix B).

But this verticality should not be seen as resulting from capitalist strength only. It also comes out of an important socialist weakness, effectively counteracted by the People's Republic of China until the death of Mao Zedong. The weakness consists in the frequent inability to have a good answer to the question: "After the satisfaction of basic

needs, what?" For that reason there may be some kind of phase movement at work here—at first a "puritan" phase, where cooperation may
maximally be of the A type, followed by a second phase when basic
needs have been satisfied and some kind of "new class" has emerged,
even vast masses of them, or "middle classes." At that time one proceeds
to cooperation of type B. Of course, preceding all that is a phase zero
of rupture, perhaps of economic boycott brought upon the emerging
socialist country by capitalist countries sufficiently unenlightened not
to understand that for socialism to be built this kind of rupture is
welcome, even essential (and so materialistic in their smugness that
they underestimate the power of ideas and faith).[9]

What would be the socialist counter-strategy to avoid this kind of
penetration? Evidently, one or more out of three—to close the country
completely, to see to it that no new class emerges capable of articulating
such individualistic and frivolous demands (for instance, for private
cars, the standard article in this faith), and by trying to lead society
away from the path of consumerism toward some other path (for example, to build a new type of society with "politics, not economic and
technology, in command").

China was practicing all three policies at the same time.[10] It was
interesting to see how both the United States and the Soviet Union
were expecting China's "experiment" to break down, because they both
believed in some kind of unilinear theory of history—history being the
process that they themselves had been through and were at the fore-
front of. Thus, the United States would say that this is what one may
find at below $100 in GNP per capita; wait until the average comes
up to $500! In the Soviet Union they would say that this is the typical
Stalinist phase of sacrificing consumption for building an economic
infrastructure; wait until the Brezhnev phase comes! They may both
have been right. But then they may also have been wrong. History is
not unilinear, the tracks are no longer necessarily laid by societies in
the West. China may also in her zigzag manner be paving the road for
some new type of society that is less materialistic,[11] even if the present
phase may not look like that.

Is there no other way in which trade ties may expand? Yes, if we
get away from the assumption underlying the preceding analysis,
namely, that the capitalist partner is technologically advanced and has
a strong economy, and that the socialist partner is the opposite of this.
There are weak capitalist countries; in fact, most of them are, as that
is what the Third World mainly consists of. There could be socialist
countries that have very advanced technology and strong economies—
either because they have been socialist for a long period of primary
accumulation (evidently the case with the Soviet Union) or because
they were quite advanced capitalist countries and only then turned
socialist. Of the latter, the only case so far is the German Democratic

**Table 2.3**
**Exchange Partners between Capitalist and Socialist Economies**[a]

| Capitalist | Socialist | |
|---|---|---|
| | Technologically Weak | Technologically Strong |
| Technologically Weak | C | 1st phase: D<br>2nd phase: E |
| Technologically Strong | 1st phase: A<br>2nd phase: B | F |

[a]The letters are defined in Table 2.2.

Republic. But these cases may come—for example, in the form of "green socialism" from among the small countries in North-Western Europe—because of the other types of dissatisfaction with capitalism (not that it fails to satisfy basic needs of those in the periphery classes or the periphery countries of the system, but that it counteracts all kinds of nonmaterial needs for creativity, togetherness, joy, freedom of more subtle kinds, self-realization, etc.).[12]

And that leads us to a new set of possibilities (Table 2.3). Everything changes the moment the two systems are, roughly speaking, at the same level of technological sophistication and can exchange raw materials with each other, or semiprocessed or manufactured goods (C and F in Tables 2.2 and 2.3). This situation may now gradually be obtained in several parts of the world. Thus, the Soviet Union and the Eastern European socialist countries may be inferior to the most advanced capitalist economies but not to the capitalist countries in Southern Europe (Greece) or around the Mediterranean in general (this would have been more obvious had *Occitanie* been independent of Paris and *Mezzogiorno* of Rome). Hence, in that area considerable growth in this type of exchange, roughly speaking, at the same level of sophistication, can be expected. Since the exchange is much less problematic than the A, B, D, and E possibilities, we would expect them to be accompanied by considerably higher levels of political leverage, not in the sense of one party dominating the other, but in the sense of harmonious relations that might benefit both parties and world peace.[13]

The same argument applies to socialist countries that used to belong to the Third World (a term we use as a political-economic concept, not as a geographic concept). They might trade with their neighbors, again focusing by and large on intra-sector rather than inter-sector trade. When the U.S. blockade against Cuba—so absolutely essential in helping Cuba to build a socialist economy that could not be eroded through the mass influx of consumer goods, sending the consumers as economic-political refugees to the goods rather than vice versa—ultimately is lifted,[14] one might expect much more trade between Cuba and her neighbors than the present trickle. But, and the same would certainly apply to the Korean case, the condition would have to be that no country tries to make the other country economically dependent, or lets itself slide into dependency.

The latter is problematic because capitalist thinking is so primitive on this point. There is trade today, even joint ventures, between strong socialist and weak capitalist countries, as exemplified by the Soviet-Indian case, typically of the D and E varieties. But the Soviet Union was also doing the same with China, and the result is well known—complete rupture, possibly because China had a socialist ideology and saw the danger signals of dependency.[15] But India and most other poor Third World countries in the capitalist Periphery are not so well equipped with the same warning mechanism: if they were, they would not have remained in the capitalist Periphery but would have done something about it. The alternative is not necessarily socialist, but could also be complete isolation (for example, Burma) or efforts to get into the capitalist Center by exploiting others, as the states of the Organization of Petroleum Exporting Countries (OPEC) may be seeking or as India tries to do in her own orbit.

The Soviet Union naturally turned to India after having "lost" China, causing obvious resentment in China. From India's point of view what happens is concealed by the thin veil of nonalignment ideology, trading with the capitalist powers *and* with the socialist powers, balancing one against the other. As a capitalist country, India still believes in the doctrine of comparative advantage; being accustomed to being the periphery of one, a transition toward being the periphery of the other may not be that difficult. Needless to say, we do not believe that situation to be stable, for the same reasons as in connection with trade of types A and D. It should be added, though, that if types A and D are really of short duration, if they prove to be beneficial and do not lead into accelerating dependency on spare parts and new technology, they are probably very positive. Usually that depends on the ability of the leadership to make use of capitalist goods to produce more capital goods at home.

Hence, our conclusion is in favor of trade of types A, C, D, and F, and considerable skepticism when it comes to the other types if the purpose of coexistence is not merely to obtain trade benefits. Symmetric trade, not asymmetric, is what is needed if some kind of harmonious

**Table 2.4**
**Partners in Capitalist and Socialist Systems of Hegemony**

|  | Social Imperialism | |
|---|---|---|
| Capitalist Imperialism | Center Country | Periphery Country |
| Center Country | US-SU (EC-SU) (J-SU) | |
| Periphery Country | | many possibilities |

structure is to be built. The relevance to the case of Korea is clear. South Korea's proposed joint ventures with the North need to be developed into a more complete package that will bring real economic development for both North and South. Raw materials need to be exchanged for raw materials, capital goods from the North for raw materials from the South and vice versa, and finished products should be traded for finished products. All of these ideas were on the table during the inter-Korean talks in 1984 (Korea, 1984). Agreement on the overall economic vision was absent because a political consensus, such as one in favor of a neutralized Korea, was lacking.

## POLITICAL RELATIONS BETWEEN THE TWO SYSTEMS

Let us now reflect on political relations between the two systems, interpreting "politics" relatively broadly. In international politics we do not expect much cooperation between the two systems in general terms. After all, there are different images of what the world ought to be. But this is as long as we use the terms "capitalist" and "socialist" without any qualification. The picture changes immediately when we look at capitalism and socialism at present as hegemonial, even imperialist, systems where countries have positions (Table 2.4).

The problem is to switch the thinking from the economic to the political sphere. We have pointed out above that there can be economic cooperation between the socialist center and the capitalist periphery because they may be technologically more or less at the same level (capitalism came first and is perhaps technologically more innovative). At least we can build trade patterns around an assumption of that type. But politically the field is rather dangerous. The global context does not permit much political cooperation between the Soviet Union and Norway until there are some fundamental changes either in that context or inside these countries (and even then, as the case of Portugal 1974–76 clearly showed, the pattern is fraught with danger).

But the other combinations are filled with potential for political cooperation. At the top is the most conspicuous one—what the Chinese refer to as superpower hegemony, which might at times be seen as cooperation based on a common interest to preserve the hegemonial system.[16] Since the hegemonial systems derive some of their legitimacy from exchanges of threat postures, increasingly destructive capacity of the war machineries on either side, etc., one possible line of cooperation would be to maintain the threat, as with the price of oil ("neither too high, nor too low"). In other words, the basic point is that there may be common interests even overshadowing the conflicts, both of interest and of value, between capitalism and socialism.

If true at the top of the systems, our conclusions should be even more applicable at the bottom to a case like Korea. There is objectively a common interest in becoming more autonomous of the superpowers. When the objective interest is not reflected in concrete cooperation (except to some extent in the European context), it is because the hegemonial systems are still intact and the superpowers see to it that such moves are not made, *and* because the pattern of superpower hegemony has not yet crystallized sufficiently for this type of Center-Periphery contradiction to mature. We would imagine that to happen in the years to come, which means that there could be some potential for political cooperation across the system-border for political leaders able to seize the opportunity. At the same time, countries particularly well suited for some type of economic cooperation would not be expected to turn each other into a dependent relationship. The best example today is probably the nonaggression treaty between Bulgaria and Greece, an example that could be copied in the Korean case.

However, political interaction is not only shaped by the global context but as much or more by the internal situation, which in turn is to some extent contingent upon the economic configuration inside the country. More particularly, most countries today tend to develop highly authoritarian regimes, especially the socialist countries and the countries in the vast capitalist Periphery (the largest exception until June 1975, was India, and then it took only a day's political work to abolish a relatively democratic regime). Democracy, in parliamentary or presidential forms, is almost only found in the capitalist Center, partly because the social classes have shared the spoils from centuries of external imperialism, co-opting the working classes into complicity by giving them some measure of political power through voting, and economic security through various types of welfare state measures (the social democrats excel at this). But in the world at large the authoritarian regime, usually by the military directly or indirectly (notably in the socialist countries) is the rule, and the two Koreas are hardly exceptions.

The reasons why socialist and periphery capitalist countries become authoritarian differ, however. The socialist countries try to withdraw from some aspects of the world capitalist system, which then tries to reintegrate them with all kinds of methods, including force—and this evidently plays up to authoritarian forces inside. But even without that external factor, an authoritarian regime is likely to come about in a certain phase because of the rules of the socialist economic game. Patterns of trade, market behavior, production for demand and profit—all the individualist competitiveness of capitalism—are not easily uprooted and will easily be regenerated unless some other system more appealing to human beings can take solid root. More particularly, subordinating individual economic behavior to the rules of the system in practice means clamping down on black markets, on smuggling, and on the "open door" through which inhabitants with the means to do so escape in order to enjoy the freedom of consumption denied them at home.

Instability will generally originate from the better off. The system is usually capable of satisfying the needs of the masses and of providing them with an existence that, for them, compares very favorably with the (periphery) capitalism that preceded it. Many socialist countries have therefore come to the conclusion that it is much better to let the well-to-do go—as Cuba did.[17] But the pattern of authoritarian rule remained, particularly when the country was a part of a system built by the Soviet Union with small groups (bridgeheads for the Soviet Union) keeping themselves in power by means of bayonets and tanks. Thus, North Korea has remained authoritarian since the end of War War II. But under Soviet leader Mikhail Gorbachev authoritarian socialism seems now to be unraveling, and that will probably also apply to North Korea.

In the capitalist countries of the periphery the instability that authoritarian regimes try to control emanates from a combination of unsettled elites (particularly students and young intellectuals) and exploited masses. Much of the control consists in trying to weaken them singly, seeing to it that they cannot join forces in an alliance that might topple the system.[18] Why the "unrest"? For the simple reason that capitalism in the Periphery does not fit the bill. It can do well along conventional capitalist dimensions, such as economic growth, export, and productivity. Elites mesmerized by such measures seem always to be equally surprised when there nevertheless is "unrest," and resort to explanations in terms of subversion and terrorism to solve their own cognitive problems in a politically acceptable way.

However, when periphery capitalism is judged in terms of nonelitist, socialist measures, such as the ability to satisfy basic needs for all and the ability to make the country self-reliant (important in time of crisis and in order to be able to withstand blackmail), and in terms of participation, including the very important category of full employment, it often falls dismally short. If we add parameters of inequality (after all, if the masses stand still or decline and there nevertheless is economic growth, somebody has to "grow," namely, the elites, upper classes, urbanized sectors, including labor aristocracies), the picture looks even worse.

As a consequence, the country will go through waves of extreme authoritarianism to break the back of the forces trying to change it in a more socialist direction, oscillating with periodic moves in a more social democrat direction, but usually failing to understand how incompatible the socialist trend is with being a dependent economy. And we must add that the regimes also usually serve a bridgehead function for the capitalist Center, guaranteeing that they can pass their economic cycles through the country according to the old formula "investment and consumer goods in, raw materials and profits out" in return for various kinds of economic, political, and military support. The case of South Korea is instructive on these points.

Political difficulties arising from authoritarianism, left or right, are well known: They generate in either side the desire to come to the assistance of those with whom they identify, and not only for selfish reasons, in order to maintain influence. Capitalist countries are always better at identifying with elites—business executives, intellectuals, *people with a face, with individuality*—than the masses, while the elites are the ones who are in difficulty under socialism. Socialist countries will in principle identify with the masses. The point is not whether either party really feels this strongly enough to do something about it in terms of subversive activity or even invasion—to come to the assistance of repressed elites or oppressed masses, respectively. The point is that either side will think that the other side is contemplating precisely this, because so much of the rhetoric is in that direction. The authoritarian tendencies are strengthened even further, aggravating rather than solving the problems of the displaced elites in socialist countries and of the exploited masses under periphery capitalism.[19]

However, it certainly does not follow that such regimes cannot cooperate, provided they are stable enough under their authoritarianism so that neither thinks it easy to topple the other. On the contrary, they may even come to cooperate quite well because authoritarian regimes have certain basic similarities. As an example; look at Spain and Yugoslavia in the 1960s, one "capitalist," the other "socialist," both based on regimes that came into being after a civil war linked to World War II, both run by a single party, the Movimiento in one and the Communist Party in the other. If they were closer to each other and had no border problem (like Trieste), they would probably have exhibited a considerable range of cooperative policies. But one reason for this is located in the circumstances that they are both mixed systems, ruled to a large extent by technocratic elites in harmony with military and party interests— and to some extent even run by computers. In principle, one computer should be able to cooperate with another.

In the Korean case the existence of one authoritarian regime on a war footing has been used as the justification for the other to have authoritarian rule and a strong military. The masses have been told to keep quiet or instability might lead to a preemptive attack from the other side. But these myths are breaking down. The very need to have a strong military means that there must be a strong economy; technocrats, vital for defense, want a role in determining policies. Authoritarianism based on military considerations is unravelling.

The question is whether there is something inherent in authoritarian regimes that may lead to a technocratic type of regime, and the answer may be a qualified "yes." A democracy can count on so much initiative and creativity from its citizens that the country can derive some dynamism from the people, not just from the elites. The same applies to the other great participatory form of system in today's world, that of China.[20] Authoritarian regimes usually do not have this possibility, by definition, and have to substitute something for it. One possibility is *planning*, relying on experts and their formulas rather than the masses. Yet another possibility is some kind of *entrepreneurism*, letting loose a number of industrialists, constructors, landowners, etc. A third possibility is to do both which is what Spain and Yugoslavia seem to be doing, creating in a short time remarkably similar countries within different ideological frameworks. It should be added, though, that this would not work with *totalitarian* countries, which are shaped in all details according to some master plan emanating from a very almighty center, and the cog wheels do not easily connect.

Thus, meeting in the middle somewhere, the interests may coincide sufficiently for political cooperation to emerge on top of economic cooperation over a wide range of sectors. But it should be added that the price is considerable to the purists, neither pure capitalism nor pure socialism. This is actually the familiar convergence thesis, and what we have tried to add here are two elements: (1) we do not think that this development is inevitable, as evidenced by countries in the capitalist Center and by the complexity of China, and (2) one possible mechanism is through the intermediary of authoritarian, particularly military regimes—and since the military are about the same all over the world (except the People's Liberation Army of China in a certain period) and tend to run countries much as they run armies (a mixture of planning and entrepreneurism), the outcome has to be relatively similar. The relevance to Korea is obvious.

What forms will this political cooperation between authoritarian regimes of either variety take? There will be exchanges of heads of state, top-level meetings, declarations, and projects, but not too much real activity, since it takes active popular participation to arrive at deeper patterns of cooperation. Authoritarian plans tend to remain paper plans. It only takes the refusal of one of the parties to let its population participate actively in cooperation for the stale, establishmentarian character of these projects to prevail. In all probability this is what will happen to much of the noneconomic cooperation between East and West in Europe as long as the authoritarianism of the Soviet Union remains—at the same time as the West will continue to exploit the East economically (according to formula B noted above).[21] The initial cooperation of North and South Korea will be similar. Skeptics will find this prospect considerably short of the ideal. Enthusiasts will point out that it is preferable to cold war, not to mention hot war. They are, of course, both right.

But what would that more ideal form resemble? We have in mind a situation that does not obtain in the world today but might exist in the future: two participatory countries, one capitalist with parliamentary democracy, the other socialist with a participatory system more like what *may be* emerging in China and in Cuba. The countries would have to be technologically at about the same level, or at least agree not to use any discrepancy as a tool for dominance. Both countries would have to permit considerable mobility of their citizens in and out, which would only be possible if the economic levels are not too different, and the political grievances of groups in one country or the other are not too obviously legitimate.

Under these circumstances a broad range of cooperation should be possible. The citizens of both countries could even benefit, conceivably, from the tremendous enrichment of life that stems from diversity, for example, by living sometime in one, sometime in the other (which, of course, is rather different from the bland eclecticism of the two ideal regimes mentioned above). If, in addition, they could find each other in joint resistance against big-power hegemony, that could add some impetus to the cooperation, even make a virtue out of political necessity. And if, in addition, the two countries border on each other and are populated by people belonging to the same nation, separated by superpower politics, divided between families, within families, between individuals, within individuals...

## CONCLUSION

So it remains only to add the obvious: these aforementioned conditions do not exist in Korea today. But one day they may, and it may be useful even in the darkest periods to maintain a vision of a more desirable future. One thing we know with certainty: No situation in the world lasts forever, including the unfortunate situation in which the Korean people find themselves. One aspect of that situation, incidentally, is Western ideologies. They are alien—hence, Koreans are alienated in different ways, not only divided. Could that fact serve as a unifying force, shared bitterness at being a pawn in an East-West conflict and a superpower conflict not of their own choosing?

In an earlier article, prompted by the famous July 4, 1982, communique, a future neutralized Korea was explored in some detail.[22] Not much has actually happened since that time; the situation has proved to be relatively stable. Korea is still divided by that line drawn during the night August 10–11, 1945, by then Colonel Dean Rusk, who had about 30 minutes to do the job. Evidently, the Americans were surprised that the Soviets accepted. The promise from Cairo on December 1, 1943, that Korea should become independent "in due course," has certainly not been fulfilled.

Nevertheless, there are perhaps some points in a more positive direction: (1) Much time has passed since the war of 1950–53. Those who experienced that shock are still in power but may not be so much longer. We are approaching T + 40 conditions. (2) At the very top there is a change of leadership in the South; when there also is a change in the North, that might loosen up the situation. Obviously, Kim Dae Jung is the man who could carry the process of association (a better term than "unification") a great step forward. He is not President, but he is at least the leader of the opposition in parliament. (3) Both Koreas are doing relatively well within the two frameworks set (see Table 2.1). This may lead to a productive self-confidence. But they are not yet willing to see each other as something positive. (4) The world system would prefer not to have Korea as one additional powder keg. Moreover, with decreasing tension in the world along traditional East-West lines, decreased tension in Korea is also to be expected.

But then there is a negative factor—the general neglect of the Korea question in a world that has so much else to bother about. When people in the Atlantic area talk about the East-West conflict, they tend to think that it is solely in the Atlantic hemisphere. There is a general tendency to hold Koreans in low esteem and to neglect the issue.[23] In short, we shall still have to wait for some time for the neutralized

Federal Republic of Koryo—or something like Nordic relations among the parts of Korea.

## NOTES

1. For some of the general theory of this see the introductory chapter of Galtung and Lodgaard (1970) and Galtung (1980: Ch. 2).
2. For an exploration of these ideologies, see Galtung (n.d.-d).
3. For more on this see Galtung (n.d.-b).
4. Probably the best book on transnational corporations is Barnet and Muller (1974).
5. The Economic Study Group of the Goals, Processes and Indicators of Development Project has been concerned, for some time, with the general idea of exploring different types of negations of capitalism; a book on an alternative economics is now in the making.
6. For a survey of some of these, see Galtung (1978: Ch. 8).
7. Which, of course, is what imperialist capitalism is about (Galtung, 1980: Ch. 13). Of course, processing of raw materials may also be on the spot, in economic free zones, etc.
8. Romania does that in bilateral technical assistance programs; the Soviet Union demands of its UN experts a payment formula whereby they retain only what corresponds to their salary at home.
9. Some of this is explored in Galtung (1980: Ch. 7).
10. See Galtung and Nishimura (1974).
11. See Galtung (n.d.-b).
12. This is where the alternative styles of life movement enters the picture (cf. Galtung, n.d.-a).
13. Whether this opportunity is really made use of is another matter.
14. The 1980 outflux of people, however, must also be seen in other perspectives. No doubt it was also used quite skillfully by the Cubans as an act of revenge.
15. They needed another concept of imperialism, though, as the Soviet economic imperialism probably was not that important (cf. Galtung, n.d.-c).
16. See the analysis of Chinese foreign policy in Galtung and Nishimura (1974).
17. See Galtung (1980: Ch. 7).
18. See Galtung (1978: Ch. 4).
19. Of course, it is also in the interest of the hegemonial powers in both systems that all these countries are authoritarian since that makes it possible to rule either part of the world through the elites.
20. Whether it is as participatory today as in the 1980s is another question. My own impression is that during the cultural revolution there was more, not less, political debate, and now there is considerably more economic freedom, both as consumer and as producer.
21. Poland's indebtedness to the West is a good example, because of—among other reasons—deteriorating terms of trade. See Galtung (1980: Ch. 2).

22. See Galtung (1980: Ch. 5).
23. See the excellent analysis by Sakamoto (1978).

## REFERENCES

Barnet, Richard J., and Muller, Ronald E. (1974). *Global Reach.* New York: Simon & Schuster.

Galtung, Johan. (1978). *Peace and Social Structure, Essays in Peace Research,* Vol. 3. Copenhagen: Ejlers.

———. (1980). *Peace Problems: Some Case Studies, Essays in Peace Research,* Vol. 5. Copenhagen: Ejlers.

———. (n.d.-a). "Alternative Life Styles in Rich Countries," *Papers* (No. 29), Chair in Conflict and Peace Research, University of Oslo.

———. (n.d.-b). "China After Mao," *Papers* (No. 61), Chair in Conflict and Peace Research, University of Oslo.

———. (n.d.-c). "Social Imperialism and Sub-Imperialism," *Papers* (No. 22), Chair in Conflict and Peace Research, University of Oslo.

———. (n.d.-d). "Alternative Life Styles in Rich Countries," *Papers* (No. 29), Chair in Conflict and Peace Research, University of Oslo.

Galtung, Johan, and Lodgaard, Sverre, eds. (1970). *Cooperation in Europe.* Oslo: University of Oslo.

Galtung, Johan, and Nishimura, Fumiko. (1974). *Learning from the Chinese People.* Oslo: University of Oslo.

Harrison, Selig. (1987). "The 'Great Follower': Kim Il Sung Promotes a Chinese-Style Open-Door Policy," *Far Eastern Economic Review,* 138 (December 2): 36–38.

Korea, Republic of. (1984). *Inter-Korean Economic Talks: A Sign of Thaw?* Seoul: Korean Overseas Information Service.

Sakamoto, Yoshikazu. (1978). *Korea as a World Order Issue.* New York: Institute for World Order.

# 3     The Functionalist Approach to Korean Reunification

### Michael Haas

## DIVIDED PEOPLES IN INTERNATIONAL AFFAIRS

Unification of divided peoples has been a motivating force in international relations for millenia, though the intensity of the drive for unification increased in the nineteenth century with the rise of nationalistic sentiments triggered by the Napoleonic wars. Such writers as Giuseppi Mazzini (1907) called for the unification of such countries as his native Italy as a method through which the peoples of the world could achieve their own destiny. Mazzini's nationalism was linked with the rise of romanticism, that is, the glorification of the root cultures of the peasants and shopkeepers, and hence had a fundamentally democratic ideological underpinning. The rise of nationalism and the spirit of democracy, thus, delegitimized the imperialist and dynastic rulers. Although Mazzini preferred peaceful unification, and Prussian Chancellor Otto von Bismarck felt that the need for the industrialists of Berlin to sell their products to a wider market meant war, they both agreed that national states would be inherently more peaceful, as those who form a common culture would always yearn to be together.

The eventual success of nationalism throughout the world is an accepted fact of contemporary politics. Very few cases of colonies and divided peoples exist today. The current examples of China, Cyprus, Germany, Ireland, Korea, Samoa, and Yemen are usually taken for granted as exceptions to the rule. But we continue to hear about the plight of divided peoples without separate sovereignty, such as the Armenians, Kurds, and the Palestinians of the Middle East as well as the Moros of the former Sulu Sultanate, who are located in Philippine

Mindanao, Malaysian Sabah, and the Sulu archipelago between these two territories. Koreans, meanwhile, are divided not only on the peninsula but live in both China and the Soviet Union. The colonies of the Malvinas Islands and New Caledonia are among the last vestiges of colonial rule. And the plight of various ethnic groups in Burma and India, Indians in Fiji, and Tamils in Sri Lanka have to be added to our list along with many other cases of peoples seeking to control their own destiny. Problems keep popping up, and the underlying generalization of the inevitability of unification under certain conditions seems immediately to come to our consciousness. Before charting such an optimistic view of the fulfillment of the dreams of Mazzini and others, it will be useful to note the key factors accounting for success and failure and unification. But there is some dispute on this question in academic circles; we have competing theoretical approaches and disparate judgments on the prospects for unification in particular cases. The initial task of this chapter is to review these theories and to identify the nature of the disagreements.

## THEORIES OF INTEGRATION AND UNIFICATION

The concept of political unification is central to theories of political integration, which speculate on factors accounting for the development of peaceful linkages between countries and peoples. Although interest in peaceful linkages can be traced to the various plans for peace of Dante, the duc de Sully, Immanuel Kant, and others, modern social science theorizing about political integration can be traced to the year 1946, when British Prime Minister Winston Churchill delivered a speech in Zurich, urging the development of "some kind of United States of Europe." The follow-up to Churchill's address was an increase in enthusiasm for the concept of European integration as a pathway to peace, and academic researchers began to construct theories that might advance the goal of European political unification, with European economic integration as a preliminary step.[1]

Theories of integration may be classified with reference to stages in the process of achieving greater harmony between peoples and states. Some scholars focus on *preconditions*, that is, on elements that are required before integration can move from stage I to stage II, from stage II to III, and so forth. A second focus is on *transaction flows*, that is, the rise and fall of trends in integrative behavior over time or over space, the latter concern consisting of an identification of subclusters of countries with dense patterns of interaction. A third focus is on the *development of integrative processes* because of, or in spite of, the volume and percentages of international interactions and/or the presence of so-called preconditions. The third mode of analysis asks whether co-membership in alliances leads to increased integration or decreased integration—and why.

Some of the initial criticisms of integration theory focused on its Eurocentrism, that is, its relevance to Europe and irrelevance elsewhere. Various preconditions to the formation of political or economic integration tended to be set forth by such scholars as Karl Deutsch (1953, 1954) and Ernst Haas (1958, 1964, 1966), and developed countries were predicted to be more likely to be successful in achieving integration. Amitai Etzioni (1965), on the other hand, felt that developing countries might be more successful at political integration because they have fewer vested interests in a nonprosperous status quo. Roger Hansen (1969), while agreeing with Etzioni, noted three specific problems. First of all, economic issues are already heavily politicized in the Third World, so it is absurd to predict that an economic union can lead to a political union through gradual politicization, or so Hansen argued; instead, developing countries must depoliticize economic issues as a precondition to the success of economic unions. Second, the superpowers hamper the freedom of Third World countries to act by penetrating their economic and political systems. Third, integrative efforts will not be possible so long as developing countries are still engaged in nation building.

Additional research on Latin American efforts at integration by Ernst Haas and two co-authors tends to support the compatibility of conclusions regarding Europe and Latin America (Haas and Schmitter, 1966; Barrera and Haas, 1969). Michael Haas (1985) and James Schubert (1978), meanwhile, find that the technioeconomic functionalism of David Mitrany (1966) is most descriptive of integrative progress in Asia, where relatively unobtrusive, functionally specific intergovernmental organizations have been far more successful than politicized forums. Meanwhile, a style of negotiation, known as the "Asian Way," has supplied an important element in functional theory by indicating that the most promising form of discussion between countries seeking to improve relations begins with areas of agreement, moves to areas of ambiguity, but scrupulously avoids stating contentious issues (Haas, in preparation).

A moment's reflection will suffice to demonstrate the new relevance of integration theory for contemporary Third World efforts. Hansen's three points no longer apply. First of all, economic union is not the objective of groups of Third World states; instead, the age of the New International Economic Order (NIEO) has dawned, and Third World countries seek to advance their own economic self-interest vis-à-vis the First World by joint cooperative efforts, such as those exemplified by the increased prices declared by the Organization of Petroleum Exporting Countries in the 1970s. Second, it is the very dependent status of the Third World that prompts attention to the collective need for a less dependent status. And, third, the era of exclusivist nationalism is largely over; no Third World country is strong enough to bring about prosperity on its own, so economic cooperation among developing countries (known as ECDC) is currently the most prominent element of NIEO, as the First and Second Worlds have failed to give any realistic support to the aims or projects of NIEO.

Summarizing at this point, we note that greater levels of political integration may be arrayed on a continuum that extends from increased contact between adjacent states (low-level integration) to political unification (high-level integration), with many intermediate levels. While Deutsch's students have tended to focus on such low-level phenomena as trade, tourist traffic, news media attention, and the like, the concerns of most other scholars have been on the use of intergovernmental organizations as facilitators or arenas for joint action. The findings have been limited to analyses based on a few cases, so there is no definitive set of propositions in the literature as yet. Nevertheless, there is general agreement that a high degree of low-level informal contact can facilitate the development of higher levels of integration; at the same time, whenever a new integrated effort is agreed to by elites of various countries, one result may be greater social communication. Hence, governmental leaders need not await higher levels of tourism, trade, and the like before agreeing to cooperate together; but the greater the informal contact among citizens of two countries, the more likely it will be that their leaders will collaborate.

## FUNCTIONALIST POSSIBILITIES FOR KOREA

Given various proposals for Korean unification, we can evaluate the potential for achievement of this objective within the framework of the various paradigms of integration discussed above. Clearly, we must look at both attitudinal and material factors, at low-level as well as high-level elements.

### Attitudinal Factors

Attitudinally, there is much official consensus on the desire for unification. Korean elites articulate endorsements of unification in principle. The peoples of North and South are also in support, including members of the various political parties in the Republic of Korea, though there is also skepticism as well. Thus, the Mazzini-type factors are favorable to unification.

Nonetheless, academic scholarship is universally pessimistic on the attitudinal prospects for Korean unification. The reasons are fourfold.

One of the reasons for pessimism is that a new generation is arising in North and South which has lived under divided rule longer than under unified rule. The generation of 10 million Koreans of divided families will be dead before long, and the pressure to reunite families will correspondingly cease. So long as the public desires unification in such practical terms as the need for family reunions, the pressure will continue; when this pressure is gone, the issue will be less attitudinally urgent, which perhaps accounts in part for the lack of discussion on unification including Koreans inside China and the Soviet Union. A second attitudinal consideration is the perception that Southerners are somehow different from Northerners. In June 1975, South Korean Prime Minister Kim Jong Pil reportedly said, "We cannot look upon the Northern Communists as of the same race as ourselves."[2] This kind of thinking tends to legitimize division, and perhaps that was its aim, as it is not a documented assertion of fact. A third attitudinal factor is the lack of cordiality that characterizes official communications between North and South, whether through propaganda barbs or at the conference table in Panmunjom (cf. Henderson, 1987). Mutual trust in negotiations requires showing respect for one's interlocutor; the converse, present even during various academic conferences, hardens bargaining positions to a point of nonnegotiability. A fourth consideration is the belief that elites back unification for political reasons in public while opposing such efforts in private as contrary to the status quo, which allocates power to their respective interests on both sides of the DMZ. On balance, however, attitudinal factors are favorable to unification; otherwise there would not be conferences on Korean reunification. But if the Korean people want unification, the question is, "On whose terms?" At present there is no compatibility of elite values and no mutual responsiveness, two factors often thought necessary for success in integrative efforts between nations. But this is in part because there is so little communication.

We therefore turn to communication and other material factors that might lead in the direction of unification. We find that they are present to only a very limited degree. There is almost no contact between North and South, although there have been about 135 Red Cross meetings since 1953. The borders are tightly controlled, militarized, and patrolled. Obviously, progress toward unification in keeping with functionalist models requires a higher level of communication in both qualitative and quantitative terms. Qualitatively, the two Koreas need to agree upon at least one common goal. As a starter, the goal of a detente seems obvious. Quantitatively, there needs to be more interaction not only to symbolize a recognition of common values but also to produce further pressures for tension reduction. Without some sort of detente betwen North and South at the highest levels there will be very little progress at other levels. Integration theory sees unification as an advanced state in a continuum or process: federation might exist before full unification, confederation before federation, a detente before confederation, and tension reduction before a detente. The agenda of tension reduction must be addressed long before we can hope to bring about reunification.

Since material preconditions do not exist for Korean unification, an infrastructure of communications between North and South needs to be constructed. Accordingly, we must review possibilities for increased interaction in light of the goal of managing tensions on the Korean peninsula. "Integration" means the establishment of stable, peaceful relations between countries; tension management is a precondition to a detente, which would be the starting point toward Korean integration or unification. As soon as a detente is reached, a step-by-step program, such as the one proposed by Johan Galtung (1972), would be appropriate. But we are at a more basic stage in relations on the Korean peninsula. Since tensions need to be reduced, increased transactions may serve the objective of tension reduction. In other words, we need to develop functional theory into detente theory in order to gain insights to apply to the Korean case.

## Political Arenas for Interaction

There are at least four arenas for interaction (Table 3.1). In the political arena the four hundred and thirty-eighth meeting of the Korean Military Armistice Commission (MAC) in early August 1987, was yet another reminder of the fact that there has been no breakthrough on efforts to negotiate a peace settlement in Korea. The scene was of four North Korean generals flanked by a Chinese military officer on one side and a UN Command consisting of two South Korean generals, an American rear admiral, and a British and a Thai military officer listening to tiresome rhetoric. About all that has been agreed upon in these spectacles is the size of the table flags, the agreement on 20 minute recesses at three-hour intervals, and what color armbands for various personnel to use in the Joint Security Area. This ritualized confrontation is good theater but has not yet played on Broadway. Graduated initiatives for tension reduction are needed, with unilateral gestures initially in order to build up mutual trust. Based on the success of the USA-USSR detente in the 1960s, such moves as a weapons freeze, reduction of foreign troops, and other dramatic de-escalatory moves would have to be reciprocated to be meaningful in an overall scenario (cf. Osgood, 1962). We have seen that President Ronald Reagan's policy of supplying vastly increased aid to the Republic of Korea means that North Korea can no longer rely on China for military assistance; dor-

Table 3.1
Arenas for International Interaction

|  | Type of Interaction | |
| --- | --- | --- |
| **Arenas** | **Formal Interaction** | **Informal Interaction** |
| Political | negotiations | reciprocated unilateral actions |
|  | exchange of delegations | conversations at diplomatic receptions |
| Economic | trade involving state trading companies | corporation-to-coporation trade |
|  |  | third-country trade (X to Y to Z) |
|  |  | smuggling |
| Cultural | exchanges of artists, musicians | viewing televised cultural performances |
| Social | athletic competition between representatives of two or more countries | academic conferences involving scholars from various countries |

mant relations between Pyongyang and Moscow came alive after Reagan entered the White House, and the Soviet Union is now far more involved in Korean affairs than ever before. The escalatory U.S. action provoked a response that was reciprocated through increased tension. The North understandably did not enjoy having to shop for more military hardware in Moscow, and the use of North Korean ports and airfields by the Soviet Union is not a step in the direction of de-escalation. Certainly a reduction in the scope of the Team Spirit military exercises could be a beginning in a de-escalatory spiral; there is no reason to continue these enormous exercises in the belief that they are not provocative. It is noteworthy that the South has never responded positively to any suggestions or moves toward military de-escalation on the peninsula and dismissed the recent gesture concerning demobilization as one similar to a previous 150,000 demobilization of armed forces for economic development projects. There is no evidence that the South has made any counterproposals concerning arms limitations, troop reductions, establishing a nuclear weapons free zone, or a reduction in the scale of military exercises. A refusal to discuss the military realities of the peninsula is to ignore the most important issue dividing North and South. Surely there is no one so naive as to believe that progress in economic cooperation can proceed without condign efforts at demilitarization. What has happened is that the North has insisted on discussing demilitarization with the United States. In the 1970s Pyongyang did not want to discuss the subject with South Korea at all. In the 1980s the North has agreed that since troops of both Koreas and the United States are present, the three parties must together agree upon a troop reduction plan, while the South unrealistically refuses to discuss the subject so long as the United States is at the conference table. The South, in other words, has subscribed to an unusual variant of "Yankee Go Home" rhetoric in which it invites U.S. troops but pretends that military de-escalation is a matter solely to be discussed between North and South, implicitly inviting U.S. troops to leave so that its bargaining position will be more reasonable. Having your cake and eating it too is nothing new in the North-South dialog, but that is why no progress seems to emerge.

The invitation to have Kim Il Sung visit Seoul, twice issued in 1981, is consistent with the detente objective, as is the North's idea of having a conference between Deputy Prime Ministers as well as a tripartite military conference. Such formal moves need to be preceded by quiet political activity, as summitry by tradition is an occasion to sign or to discuss documents prepared with some care in advance; no agenda was associated with President Chun's invitation, so the invitation itself could only be interpreted as serving a propaganda value, which no doubt it was, reciprocated in kind by North Korea in 1986. Any objective observer can only deplore the continuing use of recrimination and rhetoric on both sides in communications between North and South. Surely it must be more than a little boring and tedious for each side to write endless denunciations of the other side and empty exercises to refute each other's proposals through faulty logic. There comes a time when this verbal foolishness must stop in the interest of a greater ideal.

Efforts of the North and South to seek de facto dual recognition for the two Koreas around the world can contribute to the building of informal networks of interaction; those posted to the same capital city abroad might be members of the same extended family, might enjoy the same food, and could easily converse in the same language at diplomatic receptions held abroad. The number of countries with diplomatic missions from both Koreas is now close to 80, but I hear no reports that the two embassies are even present at the same social functions; quite the contrary, they are instructed to avoid each other. Instead, the Rangoon bombing is remembered, and the two Koreas instruct their diplomats to avoid contacts. "Hot line" telephone links between the Foreign Ministries are used, but often for propagandistic rhetoric rather than serious communication.

U.S. recognition of North Korea, of course, is one key to the strategy of cross-recognition. The U.S. policy has been called one of "balance and reciprocity," as it says that improvements in relations between Japan and North Korea will come only to the extent that there is corresponding progress between China and South Korea, while it sees positive developments in Soviet-South Korean relations as a precondition for better relations between North Korea and the United States. The motivation for U.S. policy may be the recognition that both the USSR and the United States wanted to compete in the 1988 Olympic Games, but there are more lasting elements. The United States says that it will exchange trade offices with the North if the USSR will do the same with the South. In March 1987, U.S. diplomats received new guidelines, instructing them to make substantive responses to North Korean diplomats who initiated conversations at cocktail parties and other neutral settings, even when South Korean diplomats were not present. To show its good faith, the United States offered to modify the joint military exercises conducted with the South and to grant visas for North Koreans to visit the United States. The United States hoped that the North would open its markets for sales of U.S. food and medicine in return. In addition, the United States proposed to disarm guards, to stop all loudspeaker broadcasts, and to have mutual inspection at the Joint Security Area in Panmunjom. The South did not object to these U.S. initiatives, as it was doubtless consulted beforehand, attesting to the existence of a kind of secret diplomacy that has been acknowledged unofficially between North and South in recent years (Kang, 1987). But this beginning groundwork for a detente came to nought when radical forces arranged to bomb the Korean Air flight in November 1987, then resumed when President Roh took office in 1988.

The effectiveness of the diplomacy of both North and South is reflected in an increasing number of common memberships of the two Koreas in intergovernmental organizations, inside and outside the United Nations. These arenas give additional opportunities for dialog among diplomats who might belong to divided families before those who know each other at a personal level become too old for travel abroad. But again I know of no such coincidences in staffing of delegations. The case of the Asian African Legal Consultative Committee is instructive: South Korea was only allowed Associate Membership status until 1973, when North Korea decided to join; the two now are full Members. A second example came when the two Koreas were represented in 1979 at the annual meeting of the Directors General of

Civil Aviation, Asia and the Pacific. When the North objected to a representative from the South as a nominee for Vice Chairman of the body, one delegate moved for adjournment for lunch. After the meal the nomination went forward without objection. But the following year the body convened at Seoul without representation from the North, and the proceedings published by the host Director General of Civil Aviation presumptuously listed the delegates from the peninsula as representing "Korea," rather than "Republic of Korea," as in all previous and subsequent meetings of this body. If we count the number of international conferences held in Seoul where no invitations have been issued to representatives from the North, we have some measure of the extent to which the North may feel deliberately isolated. If the two Koreas can meet together outside the peninsula, functional bridges could more easily and more decisively be built at intergovernmental meetings on the peninsula. The South cannot expect a detente with the North while pursuing a policy of isolating and upstaging the regime in Pyongyang. Perhaps the South should reconsider its opposition to having just one Korea in the UN General Assembly. If there is one seat, representatives from North and South probably would agree on many issues and in any case could conduct a continuing dialog, even though in practical terms they might have to accept a monthly rotation between the principal delegate and alternate delegate. The functionalist logic suggests that the North's concept of one seat can be put to good use. The United States, meanwhile, agreed to approve North Korea's applications for membership in various international organizations during 1987 so long as Pyongyang showed its own good faith in efforts to reduce tensions on the peninsula, but this offer was frozen in early 1988.

It should be pointed out that the visit of President Anwar Sadat to Israel was preceded by careful academic scholarship inside Israel involving scholars from countries outside the Middle East who could travel to Egypt and therein locate supporters for detente at an informal level. The subsequent Sadat visit consummated a well-planned series of informal efforts. A similar scenario for Korea seems possible, though patience will be needed, too. Such initiatives may not be feasible, for example, until the present leaders have retired. But there appears to be no academic institution working on the problem in a serious manner, though at least 51 reunification research centers do exist (Yang, 1987: n.3). The sincerity of the North and the South on the issue of unification can certainly be gauged by this absence of scholarly planning, and we must also note that only the Asian-Pacific Dialogue, a project of the University of Hawaii Insitute for Peace, seeks a detente in Korea through such a step.

In any case, detente theory argues that better relations between international adversaries must begin with steps taken at the top. As soon as leaders agree, other forms of interaction will follow more easily, gaining a momentum of their own in due course.

## Economic Arenas for Interactions

Next, *economic* interactions need to be encouraged between North and South. At one time the South was largely agricultural, the North industrial, and the peninsula had complementary halves. Now that the South has become industrialized, and the North has advanced its agriculture, we might think of the two economies as potentially competitive today. And since the North uses state trading agencies to handle imports and exports, direct trade will necessarily have an official character. Economists, nonetheless, can review prospects for increased North-South trade in specific commodities. In 1981 the South proposed 20 projects for economic cooperation, some of which had already been suggested in the "Mutual Exchange and Cooperation" element of the North's proposal of 1980. At the inter-Korean economic talks of 1984, which both sides found quite businesslike, the South proposed to export a wide range of items with the North (Table 3.2) and vice versa. The North's list of imports from the South agreed with the latter's list of exports of steel products and textile fibers, but also included iron products, tungsten, naphtha, fish, salt, and Mandarin oranges. The North's desired exports included four on the South's import list (iron ore, coal, pollacks, and corn) plus general-purpose machine tools, magnesite, mining equipment, and rice. The proposals agreed on the need to re-establish rail linkages between North and South, to set up a South-North Economic Cooperation Committee, as well as the desirability of joint ventures for coal and iron ore, and joint fishing zones. The South wanted truck-loading yards in the DMZ, while the North proposed irrigation networks in the DMZ. There are other aspects to the proposals, of course, but the deadlock was over the North's insistence on investment before trade, the South's on trade before investment, and no one seemingly willing to accept the obvious solution of investment and trade at the same time.

One precedent is provided by the Association of South East Asian Nations (ASEAN), which had the United Nations compose a team of economists to explore prospects for increased economic cooperation among the five Southeast Asian member countries. Although the progress toward economic integration in ASEAN has been less than spectacular since the UN report was finalized in the early 1970s, what did result was a series of study groups and committees to discuss ways of implementing suggestions in the UN report. The informal interactions of these groups have in many ways been more valuable than the specific economic measures implemented thus far.

Table 3.2
Proposals for Economic Cooperation, 1984

| Issues | Proposals | |
| --- | --- | --- |
| | South's Proposal | North's Proposal |
| Desired Imports | anthracite, iron ore, pig iron, lead ingots, zinc ingots, silica sand, scrap iron, Alaska pollack, silk cocoons, red beans, corn, castor beans, medicinal herbs | iron and steel products, tungsten concentrate, naphtha, textile fibers, fish from the Southern sea, salt, Mandarin oranges |
| Desired Exports | steel and steel products, copper, aluminum products, sewing machines, power tillers, passenger cards, machinery, color TVs, motorcycles, watches, clocks, audio equipment, other consumer electronics and electrical appliances, textiles, blankets, pianos, rubber belts, industrial chemicals and pharmaceuticals | iron ore, coal, general-purpose machine tools, magnesite, mining equipment, Alaska pollack, rice, corn |
| Joint Ventures Proposed | joint fishing zones; anthracite, iron ore; color TVs, audio equipment, polyester and other textile fibers, cosmetics, pharmaceuticals; tourism, shipping | joint fishing zones; iron ore, coal in the North, tungsten and molybedium in the South; joint irrigation networks |

Source:  Korean Overseas Information Service (1984)

Although South Korea offered economic and technical assistance to the Democratic People's Republic of Korea in August 1984, an equally propagandistic offer from the North for aid to victims of a flood led to the shipment of 725 truckloads of relief goods the following month. To demonstrate good will and to call the bluff of the North, the South accepted the offer. As a result, the two Koreas were at the bargaining table. Reports from China indicate that the North was nonplussed when the South accepted the offer; its view of the South as an implacable adversary was shattered. In recent years billions of dollars of North Korean coal have been shipped to South Korea each year via Hongkong; as this triangular trade flow grows, the need for a costly go-between will diminish. In 1997 the British flag will come down in Hongkong anyway.

If we wish to look at purely informal economic transactions, we would of course turn our attention to smuggling, but that is a topic that might not get us very far in terms of official planning, though it would undeniably identify items for possible increased formal trade. So far as I know, the fish being smuggled do not object.

Once again, we await serious scholarship on the subject and suspect that no one in Korea is sincere about unification when we find so little on the subject in academic publications. Economic issues do not really preclude unification, as China's various special economic zones suggest that one country can have two economic systems. With all of its government-owned corporations, the Republic of Korea can hardly claim to be a completely free market, and the advent of Hungarian-style economic reforms throughout the socialist camp will doubtless reach North Korea in due course, blurring the distinction between the two economies even further. Party Secretary Mikhail Gorbachev's proposed free port in Vladiovostok prompted one Korean scholar (Kim, 1987) to suggest that the winds of economic freedom may blow across the ten-mile distance between Vladivostok and North Korea in the coming years, leaving the fulfillment of functionalist objectives to the dynamics of private sector initiatives.

## Cultural Arenas for Interactions

Cultural interactions are another potential avenue for progress. It should be recalled that the Russo-American detente of the late 1950s brought Soviet ballet to the United States, again as a symbol of the desire for reduced East-West tensions. In Korea, radio broadcasts already reach both sides, inflaming passions, and even loudspeakers at the DMZ have not always added to increased mutual understanding. In this age of videotapes, cultural exchanges between North and South can begin with very small steps indeed, using television to foster the sense of informal unity that the Korean people seem eager to experience. Initially, the high sensitivity toward the venue of such exchanges might argue against having an audience. The 1985 Red Cross talks resulted in an agreement for an exchange of folk art troupes, which performed at the time of the Seoul and Pyongyang talks. Although exchanges of artists and musicians might be undertaken at a formal level through intergovernmental cooperation, it might be easier to use a truly demilitarized DMZ to hold cultural events. A televised broadcast of Korean cultural events from the DMZ might simplify problems of protocol, while dramatically calling the attention of citizens and government officials alike to other possibilities. Koh Young Bok (1987) has also urged exchanges of students, professors, a joint language project, joint dance and sports teams, as well as tourist promotion, all of which are to the interest of both parts of the peninsula as well as to

Koreans in China and the Soviet Union. Competition might be an element in the initial efforts at cultural exchange, but in time everyone would appreciate the common benefits of increased cultural interaction.

## Social Arenas for Interactions

At the social level, finally, we may recall that during meetings of the Korea Military Armistice Commission, journalists and commissioned officers from both sides are allowed to cross over the Northern and Southern portions of the DMZ to chat, though security officers are not. The security officers still glare at each other, clench their fists, but no longer spit at each other. But the most humanitarian aspect of social interactions is the issue of reunion visits among members of the divided families which has became stalemated perhaps because of the fact that it was an item for high-level negotiation. The North wants the visiting zone restricted, and it insists on "free visits." Meanwhile, an exchange of letters could be taking place. The 1984 Red Cross talks resulted in an agreement for reunion visits among villagers, and about 100 persons met kinfolk at the time of the Pyongyang and Seoul talks. But if leaders of North and South use the telephone to talk to each other, why not the people as well?

The main event in social interactions could have been the Summer Olympics at Seoul in 1988. We recall "ping pong diplomacy," in which a team of ping pong players symbolized efforts underway to broaden Sino-American relations. Recalling the Pyongyang table tennis competition, North Korea's proposal for a single Korean team at the Los Angeles Olympics in 1984, and the North's nonparticipation in the Asian Games of 1986, our hopes were not very high regarding 1988. Pyongyang's Friendship Games in 1989, with worldwide participation, is the response of the North to exclude the South.

In addition to sporting competition, opportunities exist for contact at neutral locations outside the peninsula, such as conferences involving scholars from North and South held in India, Japan, or elsewhere. South Koreans at the International Political Science Association at Moscow in 1979 reported crank calls from Koreans, but no joint social events were arranged by the Soviet hosts. The Pacific Science Association convened a somewhat more successful Congress at Khabarovsk in 1979, with Koreans from both halves of the peninsula among the participants.[3] Today, we hear no more about harassment of South Koreans by the North, but in 1987 the Pacific Science Congress at Seoul once again excluded the North. Current South Korean proposals for unification are based on theories of integration from Western social science; they contain a logic that may be unfamiliar to scholars and government officials in the North, who rely on a Marxist paradigm for interpreting history that may be less appreciated in the South, though functionalist elements are in proposals of the North as well. Were scholars from North and South to be present at a conference where they could expose each other to various approaches, a greater amount of understanding at the official level could percolate upward from the scholars involved.

The above are a few modest suggestions. Most have been discussed in Korea for some time. It is important for the initiative to be retained by nongovernmental persons and groups, but governments need to unfreeze their propaganda-oriented approaches toward the subject in the interest of tension reduction. More and more persons are visiting the Democratic People's Republic of Korea, and more Koreans from the North are participating in events elsewhere. The freedom of travel enjoyed by those in the Republic of Korea to go abroad also works to the advantage of functionalist possibilities for interaction in informal, unregulated arenas. As the number of potentialities for interaction increases, so must the actualities. The first and second interaction events involving citizens of North and South can only be highly politicized. The eight thousand and third such experience will be of lesser political significance.

A question therefore arises as to the catalyst for informal interactions. Clearly, much of the initiative will have to come from within the Republic of Korea. Some in the opposition parties in the South feel strongly on the subject; the party in power also has vigorous supporters for the concept of reunification. Informal discussions between the two groups might well serve to provide the necessary innovative ideas.

## CONCLUSION

In sum, there are a number of serious obstacles to Korean reunification. The first step is to encourage more dialog at the highest level by having no agenda item excluded from discussion. The South must be prepared to discuss the central issue, namely, troop maneuvers and troop strength on the peninsula, while the North must continue to display the businesslike approach that was taken at the 1984 economic talks. Thereafter, less politicized integrative activities will be possible. The high degree of politicization on all issues involving the divided peninsula has served no useful purpose. A detente is possibly within reach, but the level of rhetoric is too harsh. Diplomatic activity has picked up, but both sides need to be more flexible. More opportunities for contact in international organizations are likely to occur. Increased North-South trade is occurring. Videotapes of cultural events already exist, and they can be shared free of charge, with the South taking the first step if necessary. The trend, thus, is for more communication, not less. Institutions of higher learning, which can organize innovative North-South projects as well as conferences of scholars from North and South, exist all over the world. Small steps toward a larger goal need to be planned at this time. The middle and giant steps will come later.

The future scenario is as follows: tension reduction, detente, then unification, though the unification will have to be a formalistic compact so long as the two Koreas pursue diametrically opposed economic and political systems. Military and political talks can take place before, during, or after economic and cultural talks; functionalist theory has no set order to these events in the beginning, but political breakthroughs are needed before communications on other levels will become significant enough to spill back into further measures for detente, with some sort of unification down the road. Functionalism, after all, is neutralization on an issue-by-issue basis. As soon as a wide range of communications is taking place, discussion of appropriate methods for greater inter-country coordination of existing contacts will be the item on an agenda at a conference involving technocrats if not foreign ministers, heads of state, as well as organizations of more humble status. With a backdrop of successful integrative efforts, integrative processes can proceed as an independent pressure of its own, and such negotiations can proceed with an element of good will. Increased "coordination" from a practical standpoint, after all, is what theories of integration and unification call a higher level of "integration."

Korea has been divided for only 40 years. The unification of Germany and Italy was a dream that was pursued for nearly 1,000 years. Functionalist theory is an approach that provides short-range prescriptions for long-range goals. It is not the only theory that can be applied to the Korean case. Its balance between idealism and realism, between short- and long-range perspectives, and between optimism and pessimism is a measure of its utility both for academic theorizing and for practical statecraft.

## NOTES

1. For two summaries of empirical findings derived from research to test integration theory, see M. Haas (1974: Ch. 8) and Puchala (1981: Ch. 6).

2. Quoted in McCormack (1978: 223), which cites "Dokyumento," *Sekai*, May, 1976, p. 263.

3. Dae-Sook Suh, Director of the Korean Studies Center of the University of Hawaii at Manoa, was also in attendance.

## REFERENCES

Barrera, Mario, and Haas, Ernst B. (1969). "The Operationalization of Some Variables Related to Regional Integration: A Research Note," *International Organization*, 23 (October): 150–60.

Chung, Dae-Haw. (1980). *Toward a Pluralistic Security Community: The Relevance of Integration Theory for Divided Nations with Special Emphasis on the Case of Korea.* Philadelphia: unpublished Ph.D. diss., University of Pennsyslvania.

Deutsch, Karl W. (1953). *Nationalism and Social Communication.* New York: Wiley.

———. (1954). *Political Community at the International Level.* Garden City, NY: Doubleday.

Etzioni, Amitai. (1965). *Political Unification.* New York: Holt, Rinehart and Winston.

Galtung, Johan. (1972). "Divided Nations as a Process: The Case of Korea," *Journal of Peace Research,* 9 (4): 345–60.

Haas, Ernst B. (1958). *The Uniting of Europe.* Stanford, CA: Stanford University Press.

———. (1964). *Beyond the Nation State.* Stanford, CA: Stanford University Press.

———. (1966). "International Integration: The European and the Universal Process." In Amitai Etzioni, ed., *International Political Communities,* pp. 93–129. Garden City, NY: Doubleday.

Haas, Ernst B., and Schmitter, Philippe C. (1966). "Economics and Differential Patterns of Political Integration: Projections About Unity in Latin America." In Amitai Etzioni, ed., *International Political Communities,* pp. 259–99. Garden City, NY: Doubleday.

Haas, Michael. (1974). *International Systems.* San Francisco: Chandler.

———. (1984). "Paradigms of Political Integration and Unification: Applications to Korea," *Journal of Conflict Resolution,* 21 (1): 47–60.

———. (1985). *Basic Data of Asian Regional Organizations.* Volume 9 of *Basic Documents of Asian Regional Organizations.* Dobbs Ferry, NY: Oceana Publications.

———. (in preparation). *The Asian Way to Peace: A Story of Regional Cooperation.* New York: Praeger Publishers.

Hansen, Roger D. (1969). "Regional Integration: Reflections on a Decade of Theoretical Efforts," *World Politics,* 21 (January): 242–71.

Henderson, Gregory. (1987). "Time to Change the US-South Korea Military Relationship," *Far Eastern Economic Review,* 138 (October 22): 40.

Kang, Young Hoon. (1987). "Diplomatic Aspects of Korean Unification," paper presented at the International Conference on Korean Unification Problem Revisited, Seoul, August 20–21.

Kim, Jin-Hyun. (1987). "Economic Aspects of Korean Unification," paper presented at the International Conference on Korean Unification Problem Revisited, Seoul, August, 20–21.

Koh, Young Bok. (1987). "Social-Cultural Aspects of Korean Unification," paper presented at the International Conference on Korean Unification Problem Revisited, Seoul, August 20–21.

Korea, Republic of. (1984). *Inter-Korean Economic Talks: A Sign of Thaw?* Seoul: Korean Overseas Information Service.

Mazzini, Giuseppe. (1907). *The Duties of Man and Other Essays.* London: Dent.

McCormack, Gavan. (1978). "Reunification: Problems and Prospects." In Gavan McCormack and Mark Selden, eds., *Korea, North and South*, Ch. 12. New York: Monthly Review Press.

Mitrany, David. (1966). *A Working Peace System*. Chicago: Quadrangle.

Osgood, Charles E. (1962). *An Alternative to War or Surrender*. Urbana: University of Illinois Press.

Puchala, Donald. (1981). "Integration Theory and the Study of International Relations." In Richard L. Merritt and Karl W. Deutsch, eds., *From National Development to Global Community*, Ch. 6. London: Allen & Unwin.

Schubert, James N. (1978). "Toward a 'Working Peace System' in Asia: Organizational Growth and State Participation in Asian Regionalism," *International Organization*, 22 (Spring): 425–62.

Yang, Sung Chul. (1987). "Korean Reunification: A Comparative Perspective," paper prepared for presentation at the International Conference on Korean Unification Problem Revisited, Seoul, August 20–21.

Yu, Suk-Ryul. (1986). "Unification Strategies of South and North Korea," *Korea & World Affairs*, 10 (Winter): 776–97.

# 4    *The Nonviolence Approach to Korean Reunification*
*Glenn D. Paige*

## THE REVOLUTION OF PEACE

The great unfinished revolution of the modern world, flowing from earlier revolutions for Liberty (French and American) and Equality (Russian and Chinese) is the Revolution of Fraternity and Sorority (Peace)[1] in which descendants of the earlier revolutions and indeed all humanity must participate. The peaceful reunification of Korea can make a leading contribution to this revolution as an example to speed nonviolent transformation of global life.

Hitherto the great revolutions for Liberty and Equality have accepted the threat and use of killing force (righteous violence) as a means for initial success, subsequent defense, and attempted diffusion—contributing to the worldwide spread of militarized cultures that are legitimized in terms of peace, freedom, and economic justice.

It is becoming increasingly clear, however, that continued commitment to use and threat of lethal force by governments and their antagonists—as well as by individuals and other groups—is pathologically dysfunctional for human survival. Indeed commitment to violence is a root cause of the principal problems that cry out for solution with increasing intensity in the twilight of the twentieth century. The people of the world are slowly beginning to learn that neither true Liberty nor true Equality are possible without Peace.

This can be illustrated in three statements by a perhaps unlikely forerunner of nonviolent global transformation, the former general and president of the United States, Dwight D. Eisenhower:

*On Liberty*: In the councils of government we must guard against the acquisition of undue influence, whether sought or unsought, by the military-industrial complex. The potential for the disastrous rise of misplaced power exists and will persist. We must never let the weight of this combination endanger our liberties or democratic processes. We should take nothing for granted.[2]

*On Equality*: Every gun that is made, every warship launched, every rocket fired signifies, in the final sense, a theft from those who hunger and are not fed, those who are cold and are not clothed. This world in arms is not spending money alone. It is spending the sweat of its laborers, the genius of its scientists, the hopes of its children ... This is not a way of life at all in any true sense. Under the cloud of threatening war, it is humanity hanging from a cross of iron.[3]

*On Peace*: Indeed, I think that people want peace so much that one of these days governments had better get out of their way and let them have it.[4]

The great nonviolent teachers in history such as the Buddha, Jesus, Mohammed, Gandhi, and Martin Luther King, Jr., could hardly have expressed better the threats of violence and the needs for peaceful transformation in the present era. Have the leaders of the Democratic People's Republic of Korea, the Republic of Korea, Japan, the People's Republic of China, the Union of Soviet Socialist Republics, and other countries made comparable statements on these themes?

## FIVE TASKS FOR NONVIOLENT GLOBAL TRANSFORMATION

Five related global problems must be solved concurrently if humanity is to greet the dawn of the twenty-first century with celebration and not lamentation. These are: (1) removal of the threat to human survival posed by nuclear weapons, biochemical weapons, and other weapons of mass destruction; (2) removal of the threat to economic survival posed by violent maintenance of structures of material deprivation and by diversion of life-sustaining resources for life-taking purposes; (3) removal of threats to freedom and diversity of cultural expression that are posed by psycho-physical terror, torture, and killing; (4) removal of threats to the viability of the biosphere that result from direct violence and from related economic and industrial despoilation; and (5) the removal of lethal divisiveness among the various segments of humanity that prevents constructive cooperation in solving global problems.

Stated positively, the Revolution of Peace means the mass withdrawal of support from violence combined with principled commitment to achieving peaceful ends by nonviolent means. It means also commitment to acquiring knowledge and skills in all walks of life that will make possible a truly nonviolent world.

1. The Revolution of Peace seeks to create conditions of nonviolent common security for all humanity by transforming lethal military institutions into forms of compassionate service to human needs. Gene Keyes, for example, has argued that it is possible to transform existing military institutions to perform nonviolently ten services under three missions that are ordinarily pursued by threat and use of killing force. They are PEACE—rescue action, civic action, and colossal action (tasks requiring massive commitments of labor and technology); CONFLICT—friendly persuasion, guerrilla action, police action, and buffer action; and WAR—defense, expeditionary action, and invasion (Keyes, 1982).

2. The Revolution of Peace seeks to transform structures of economic deprivation to ensure the well-being of all. Economic transformation is to be accomplished by nonviolent means, including nonviolent revolution by the suffering millions throughout the world. This is called for by 53 Nobel Prize recipients in a little-publicized 1981 "Manifesto" in response to the "silent holocaust" of millions of preventable deaths caused by malnutrition and disease. They explain, "All of those who denounce and combat this holocaust are unanimous in maintaining that *the causes of this holocaust are political.*" (Emphasis added.) After calling upon the advantaged to take swift rescue action, they then call upon the oppressed:

> If the weak organize themselves and use the few but powerful weapons [means—GDP] available to them: non-violent actions exemplified by Gandhi, adapting and imposing objectives which are limited and suitable; if these things happen it is certain that an end could be put to this catastrophe in our time (International Foundation for Development Alternatives, 1981: 3[63].

Nonviolent action must contribute to the realization of an equitable global economy with distributive justice—responding to the needs of all—within and between nations based upon peaceful productivity.

3. The Revolution of Peace also seeks to affirm creative human diversity by removing restraints upon and by providing supports for nonviolent freedom of expression. This has been begun compassionately in the worldwide work of Amnesty International[5] which bases its efforts mainly upon provisions in the UN Universal Declaration of Human Rights such as the following:

> *Article 5.* No one shall be subjected to torture or to cruel, inhuman or degrading treatment or punishment.
> *Article 9.* No one shall be subjected to arbitrary arrest, detention or exile.
> *Article 18.* Everyone has the right to freedom of thought, conscience and religion; this right includes freedom to change his [or her] religion or belief and freedom alone or in community with others and in public or private, to

manifest his [or her] religion or belief in teaching, practice, worship and observance.

*Article 19.* Everyone has the right to freedom of opinion and expression; this right includes freedom to hold opinions without interference and to seek, receive and impart information and ideas through any media and regardless of frontiers.

No task on the agenda of nonviolent global transformation can be accomplished well by suppression of peaceful criticism and proposal of constructive alternatives. Whereas violence stifles expression of needs, nonviolence encourages their communication.

4. A nonviolent Revolution of Peace encompasses the natural environment as well as human society. It is the first revolution to seek liberation of nature as well as that of human beings. It realizes that celebration of life is impossible if the biosphere is destroyed. It seeks to restore lost vitality and to enhance peaceful uses of land, water, air, and outer space as set forth in the UN World Charter for Nature (United Nations, 1982) which declares that "nature shall be secured against degradation caused by warfare or other hostile activities" (I, par. 5) and "military activities damaging to nature shall be avoided" (III, par. 20). It seeks also realization of the recommendations for environmental management and research priorities made by an international group of scientists convened by the Royal Swedish Academy of Sciences in 1982 (Ambio, 1983). They concluded that we already have enough knowledge to stop the dangers of hazardous chemicals, processes, and wastes; depletion of tropical forests; desertification due to overgrazing; pollution by human wastes and their entrance into water resources; destruction of river basins; overpopulation and urbanization; acid deposition; species loss; destruction of the marine environment; and the fuelwood crisis.[6]

Finally the Revolution of Peace seeks to establish formal and informal institutions for cooperation in global problem-solving that are responsive to the needs of all. It seeks the peaceful, problem-solving reunification of humankind. Nonviolence unites; violence divides.

Although noted last, the creation of need-responsive processes of problem-solving is the key to nonviolent global transformation. For, as John Burton has brilliantly argued, failure to respond to universal human needs is the cause of violence (Burton, 1979). Such needs include "identity, consistency in response, stimulation, security, recognition, meaning, sense of control, and role defense." These needs are shared by all, leaders and led, rich and poor, oppressors and oppressed. Their violation leads to violent outrage. Therefore if violence and its noxious consequences are to be removed from global life, processes for problem-solving must be created in which all whose needs are unmet can participate.

## KOREA'S CREATIVE PROBLEM-SOLVING POTENTIAL

What contributions can Korea make to nonviolent global transformation? How can peaceful Korean reunification help to lead humankind away from pathological processes of behavioral and structural destruction toward affirmation of life, economic well-being, and cultural and environmental vitality? And what nonviolent global resources can Koreans call upon to assist peaceful reunification?

Korea's global problem-solving potential lies in at least three principal areas: creativity, a tradition of peacefulness, and intimate knowledge of four of the twentieth century's most dynamic and influential violence-prone nations.

The case for creativity rests upon the remarkable accomplishments achieved since 1945 in each part of the nation despite the 1950–53 wartime devastation. The emphasis placed upon the nature and value of human creativity in the *juche* philosophy is amply justified by the results of purposeful striving to realize values in both parts of the divided nation. In fact, comparison of divided Korean experience provides profound insight into the importance of human purposefulness in achieving desirable material and cultural conditions.[7]

What if the creativity already demonstrated by—and inherent in— the people of the two parts of the country were focused upon solving the problem of peaceful reunification in their own interest and as a contribution to nonviolent global transformation? The uncoerced combination of the two creativities promises creativity of a higher order than either alone has yet been able to express. One way to symbolize this is to adopt ancient yin-yang philosophical symbolism to express the combinatorial creativity (even nonviolent dialectic) of northern red and southern blue striving purposively for the welfare of all within the circle of peaceful Korean unity (Figure 4.1). The greatest challenge to Korean creativity, of course, lies in the need to transform violence-prone political and military conditions into constructive nonviolent institutions for common problem-solving and for common security— both within Korea and between Korea and its neighbors. The greater the peaceful political-security creativity, the greater the expected benefits in other areas of Korean life.

A second source of peaceful promise lies in *ingansŏng*, the life-respecting humanist roots of Korean tradition. There is no violence in the ancient creation myth of the Korean people who are said to have been produced by the union of a son of the Creator (heaven) and a bear-

**Figure 4.1**
**Nonviolent Combinatorial Creativity in Korea**

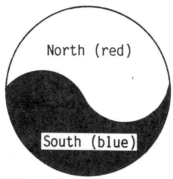

turned-woman (earth).[8] In traditional institutions civil officials ideally took precedence over military ones. Customarily Koreans did not attack their neighbors, being victims rather than initiators of military aggression. They engaged in military actions abroad only under coercion or cooptation by foreigners as by Mongols against Japan, by Japanese against China and other Asian peoples, and by Americans against the people of Vietnam.

The roots of Korean peacefulness include life-respecting indigenous values, Buddhism, Confucian ideals of influence by moral example, Christian pacifism, and Marxist humanism. These cultural roots are so strong that despite unprecedented militarization since 1945; despite wartime horrors; despite atrocities such as the Kwangju massacre of 1980, the Rangoon bomb assassinations of 1983, and the Korean Air bombing of 1987; despite idealization of revolutionary violence in the North and of counterrevolutionary violence in the South—killing is generally regarded as an unwanted and illegitimate aberration. Koreans do not accept the idea of living forever under the threat of violent coercion, either from within or from without. Neither do they seek to become one of the world's most dangerous killer nations.

Korean respect for family relations is another source of peacefulness. In ideal terms, the Korean nation (*minjok*) is a peaceful Korean family (*kajok*) writ large. With every passing year of violent division, however, the probability increases that the surviving members of millions of family members will never be reunited. A simple calculation tells the tragic story and makes a heart-tugging appeal to reason (Table 4.1).

The magnetism of family sentiment draws the Korean nation together. The greatest challenge facing Korean leaders is not to reunify the nation by force before they themselves die, but rather to achieve peaceful conditions that will permit families to reestablish relationships before death divides them forever. In the judgment of history, nonviolent family reunifications will be deemed a more meritorious

**Table 4.1**
**Aging of Divided Korean Family Members**

| Age at Division 1945 | Age Today 1988 | Future Ages | |
|---|---|---|---|
| | | 1998 | 2008 |
| 10 | 53 | 63 | 73 |
| 20 | 63 | 73 | 83 |
| 30 | 73 | 83 | 93 |
| 40 | 83 | 93 | xx |
| 50 | 93 | xx | xx |
| 60 | xx | xx | |
| 70 | xx | | |
| 80 | | | |
| 90 | | | |

Key:   xx = survival highly unlikely, 100 or over.

leadership achievement than violent national reunification accomplished by the killing and mutilation of additional millions of family members.

In addition to historical propensities, cultural values, and family sentiment, another source of Korean peacefulness is the shared experience of wartime suffering. Suffering in the North was particularly acute. This is little appreciated in the United States and in other wartime allies of the ROK, even in the South. The main reason is that the North was incessantly subjected to air attacks, day and night, throughout the three-year war. The South was never bombed. Although war would have been abolished long ago if people who suffered from it decisively committed themselves to peace, painful Korean memories of wartime suffering can be expected to reinforce natural peaceful aspirations. Furthermore, the certain destruction by war of the remarkable achievements of postwar economic reconstruction adds another factor in favor of peace.

A third contribution to Korean potential for leadership in nonviolent global transformation lies in intimate knowledge of four dynamic powers that have shaken the globe over the past century: China, Japan, the Soviet Union, and the United States. No other people have known all four on such intimate terms.

Emerging toward national independence in the late nineteenth century out of its traditional position as a Chinese tributary state, Korea was first subjected as a colony of militarily industrializing Japan, and then put into a condition of divided dependence upon socialist Russia and capitalist America, followed by intensified influence from revolutionary China and from economically expansive Japan. In less than

85 years Koreans have received powerful influences from Ching, Maoist, and post-Maoist China; from Meiji, Taishō, and Shōwa Japan; from Czarist, Stalinist, and Gorbachevist Russia; and from the United States of Wilson, Truman, and Reagan.

Undoubtedly the leaders and people of the North understand best the Soviet Union and China, while those in the South are more knowledgeable about the United States and Japan. If the two parts of the nation can pool their knowledge they can achieve extraordinary understanding of the capacities and limitations of the four great powers as contributors to nonviolent global transformation. If the Korean people can purposively use this knowledge to influence these powers for peace through processes of nonviolent politics, they can make an enormous contribution to the well-being of humankind, multiplied far beyond their own size and physical capacity. For this reason, the formation of a nonviolent policy analysis group that includes specialists from both North and South on China, Japan, the Soviet Union, and the United States deserves an early place on the agenda of peaceful Korean reunification.

## THE RELEVANCE OF KOREA'S REUNIFICATION PROPOSALS FOR NONVIOLENT GLOBAL TRANSFORMATION

The reunification proposals that are being put forth with increasing frequency and diversity by both North and South are products of Korean creativity, peacefulness, and great power understanding. They include the extraordinarily significant ten-point proposal for a "Democratic Confederal Republic of Koryo" (1980) [Appendix A], and the "Proposal for Twenty Pilot Projects for National Reconciliation and Democratic Unification" (1982) [Appendix B]. Both deserve serious discussion.[9] Already they promise important contributions to solving problems of nonviolent global transformation.

### Task 1: Achievement of Disarmament and Nonviolent Common Security

Korean proposals to create a nuclear free zone, to neutralize the peninsula, to withdraw foreign forces, to demilitarize the zone of division, to eliminate military alliances, to reduce armed forces, to demobilize militia, to organize common security institutions, to end civilian military training, and other measures deserve to be considered very seriously as contributions to global demilitarization called for in the final document of the UN General Assembly Special Session on Disarmament in 1978.[10] If Koreans can accomplish these tasks on the peninsula they can make profoundly significant contributions to the liberation of humankind from threat and use of killing force.

## Task 2: Achievement of Economic Well-Being and Justice

The Korean demilitarization proposals are also extremely important for releasing economic resources to serve pressing human needs both within Korea and abroad. They can benefit not only Koreans directly but also all those who suffer among the distant suppliers and supporters of Korean militarization. Other proposals to conduct mutually beneficial trade between the two parts of Korea, to open up transportation and communication, to establish a joint fisheries zone,, to cooperate in developing natural resources, to share technology, to improve the standards of living of all Koreans, and to promote beneficial economic exchanges with all world nations offer important possibilities for a more satisfying and just economy not only in Korea but throughout the world. Korean efforts to achieve common economic welfare in the context of nonviolent common security can contribute much to—as well as learn from—growing efforts to establish more beneficial economical relationships within and between the European Economic Community (EEC) and the Council for Mutual Economic Assistance (COMECON).

## Task 3: Achievement of Relationships that Respect and Enhance the Human Dignity of All

The Northern offer and Southern acceptance of disaster relief assistance in the fall of 1984 already has provided an important example of peaceful mutual responsiveness to human needs. Increasingly determined efforts to reunite divided families promise a highly significant breakthrough in respect for human dignity. Additional proposals for exchanges in such fields as art, science, sports, and journalism; for joint research on national history; for creation of a joint tourism area; and for travel between North and South via Panmunjom all recognize the crucial importance of the variety of ways in which the dignity of common humanity may be affirmed.

As everywhere, the path toward toleration of the expression of political views that differ from violence-based orthodoxy is a long and difficult one. The proposal to accept the existence of the political institutions of the other part of Korea without intent to destroy them by violence constitutes an important beginning. Each part will have to learn to tolerate peaceful criticism within itself as it tries credibly to claim the right to advance its views peacefully within the territory of the other. Peaceful political coexistence between and within the parts of Korea must be mutually reinforcing.

Fundamental to the achievement of freedom of expression in Korea as elsewhere will be principled commitment to the ethic of nonviolence by all. This includes both dissenters and those who seek to counter dissent. This is not just a pious ideal. If nonviolence were not the fundamental law of life, the human family and civilization itself would long ago have disappeared from the earth. Through proposals and actions that recognize the essential dignity of human life in all its aspects, Koreans can contribute greatly to the emergence of nonviolent global politics.

### Task 4: Preservation and Enhancement of the Biosphere

Koreans live in a beautiful land: peninsular earth, mountains, rivers, forests, seas, atmosphere, flowers, animals, birds, and fishes do not know that they have been divided. They are the life-sustaining heritage of the Korean people and a common treasure of all humankind. Every Korean proposal for cooperative action to preserve, restore, and enhance the natural environment against the ravages of military-industrial despoilation calls for global celebration. Such a proposal is that which calls for a joint study of flora, fauna, and the ecological system in the demilitarized zone between the present massive opposing armies. As Koreans join together to respect their environmental heritage, they must have the support of the peoples of China, Japan, the Soviet Union, and the United States as well as of other countries to succeed. Nature is not divided into nations. Recognition of the environmental unity of the Korean peninsula contributes to recognition of the ecological unity of the world.

### Task 5: Establishment of Peaceful (Need-Responsive) Processes of Problem-Solving

The Confederal proposal of 1980 has two great strengths: it affirms unity and recognizes diversity. It proposes to establish a dually constituted Confederal institution to facilitate an all-Korean approach to problem-solving. At the same time it respects the given political, economic, social, and cultural realities of the two parts and their international relationships. The problem is similar to that confronted by the United Nations: how to engage all humankind in the advancement of its own well-being, without coercion and with respect for the autonomy and dignity of its members.

The great challenge to Korean creativity is to strengthen the non-

violent need-responsive capabilities of the Confederal (or other unifying) institution, while simultaneously demilitarizing South and North,
respecting their identity, and encouraging reciprocal learning of ways
to realize the profoundly significant values of freedom and equality
that have inspired their development since 1945.

The various proposals for meetings among leaders, establishment of
communications, exchanging of missions, drafting of constitutions,
holding of elections, and for engaging foreign governments and peoples
in dialogues are all innovative efforts to create problem-solving processes that are responsive to Korean needs. That they are made at all
is evidence of aspirations to find peaceful ways to overcome division.
The fact that they are sometimes met with fear and distrust is a legacy
of experience with violent politics from which liberation must be
achieved in the Revolution of Peace.

The fact that people in the two parts of Korea are reaching out to
establish relationships between themselves, between themselves and
the four proximate powers, and with all the peoples of the Earth is an
encouraging contribution to the establishment of nonviolent processes
of global problem-solving.

## NONVIOLENT GLOBAL RESOURCES

The task of peaceful reunification poses an enormously creative challenge to the Korean people, their proximate neighbors, and to all of
humankind. Although there is a sense of venturing upon an unprecedented voyage, Koreans and others can draw upon nonviolent
resources[11] that are the common heritage of humanity to ensure success
of the journey.

Most importantly the peaceful and nonviolent traditions of Korea
need to be rediscovered and reaffirmed, from the beginnings of life on
the peninsula to the present. The development of Korean ideas on
nonviolence since national division in 1945 is an especially important
research priority. Despite all the historical violence, both glorious and
ignominious, the great story of the Korean people is life, the will to
live, and willingness to respect the lives of others. Like all humanity,
Koreans are capable of killing but are not by nature killers. This must
be lucidly affirmed as the basis for all reunification efforts. Korea
should be reunified peacefully, not because two deadly armies with
incredibly lethal foreign support are capable of exterminating them
forever, but because it always has been and always will be in the
interest of Koreans and their neighbors to live at peace with one another.

Next, Koreans should take heart from and seek to bring forth the
nonviolent cultural potentials within and across the peoples of the four

proximate powers. All should be mindful of the nonviolent Buddhist and Taoist traditions of China, the Buddhist and even Shintō pacifist traditions of Japan, the Tolstoyan and Marxist pacifist heritage of the Soviet Union, and the nonviolent movements in the United States, including the Quakers, that have struggled to influence national life since the eighteenth century. Koreans now and in the future are dealing not only with the legacy of Mao Zedong but that of Mo Tzu and Lao Tzu, not only that of Japanese militarism but that of the Sōka Gakkai and the Jinrui Aizen Kai, not only that of Lenin but that of Tolstoy, not only that of Harry S. Truman but that of Martin Luther King, Jr.

In addition Koreans need to be aware of and ready to call upon nonviolent traditions in virtually all world cultures and religions. There are nonviolent (nonkilling) Buddhists, Christians, Jews, Muslims, Marxists, and adherents of other belief systems throughout the world. The idea of nonviolence is not a monopoly of any culture, although it varies in extent of cultural influence.

Furthermore, it is important to realize that nonviolence is not some impossible dream—or philosophical-religious fantasy—but rather a value that has begun to be translated into public policy by nations with long records of violence. For example, by 1987 28 nations had completely abolished the death penalty.[12] Imagine, no more executions for actual or alleged crimes! Also by 1972, 28 nations had accepted in law the right of citizens to refuse to serve in armed forces because of belief in the impermissibility of taking human life.[13] Imagine putting the value of respect for life above the concept of required violent defense of national security or offensive military projection of national interests!

Beyond values and laws, it is important to note emergence of institutional expressions of nonviolent aspirations. For example, one of the world's most important contemporary political innovations is the rise of Die Grünen (the Greens), the nonviolent ecological movement and political party in West Germany and other countries. If Die Grünen are a First World innovation, then Solidarity in Poland and Gandhian-type movements in India and elsewhere are complementary counterparts in the Second and Third Worlds. Among many other resources are the nonviolent United Farm Workers Union led by Cesar Chavez; the institutionalization of university training for nonviolent action in the Shanti Sena (Peace Brigade) of Gandhi Rural University in Tamil Nadu, India; the existence of unarmed police in London and unarmed citizens in Japan; the example of conversion of a military industry to peaceful production provided by workers of Lucas Aerospace Limited in England; and the organization of commissions and international symposia to study the feasibility of nonviolent national defense in several Scandinavian and Western European countries.

Beyond these varied institutional innovations that are emerging in various parts of the world, it is important to note that serious efforts are being made to develop nonviolent political theories to guide constructive action. These theories eventually must replace the centuries-old doctrines of necessary and justified political-military lethality that now threaten physical, economic, psychic, and ecological survival of humankind. In the First World, Gene Sharp is developing the theory that political power rests primarily upon mass compliance, not physical force. Therefore, nonviolent political power lies in the ability to withdraw mass support from oppressive systems of exploitation, repression, and injustice (Sharp, 1973). In the Second World, theorists are developing the nonviolent aspects of Marxist-Leninist theory that make it practical to accomplish a sharp shift in class power with "virtually no bloodshed," no civil war, and no foreign military intervention (Plimak and Karyakin, 1979). In the Third World, theorists are examining the implications of Gandhian experience for nonviolent national liberation and for nonviolent revolution to uplift the lives of impoverished rural and urban masses (Zhang, 1982). Added to these efforts is an attempt to develop a new nonviolent discipline of political science from a global perspective (Paige, 1980).

The importance of these and other nonviolent global resources is not that they promise ready-made solutions to Korean reunification problems; rather, their existence provides practical confidence in human capacity to take nonviolence seriously. They demonstrate human ability to envisage and to realize nonviolent alternatives. They can stimulate and support efforts by Koreans and their friends throughout the world to create a new nonviolent Korean nation.

## CONCLUSION

The peaceful reunification of Korea contributes to—and draws upon—the Revolution of Peace that is essential for the survival and progress of humankind with liberty and equality into the twenty-first century. Korean strengths of creativity, peacefulness, and knowledge of its principal partners applied to the reunification process promise to make significant contributions to the tasks of nonviolent global transformation. These include achievement of demilitarization, economic well-being for all, respect for human dignity, preservation of the biosphere, and establishment of problem-solving processes that respond to human needs. Korean reunification efforts can benefit from the nonviolent resources of humankind from cultural values to political institutions and popular movements.

The Korean feeling that something in common unites them—despite all the violence of 40 years of divided hostility—provides one of humankind's best hopes for progress toward nonviolent global transformation in the present era. It is surely misleading to approach Korean reunification primarily in terms of fear of mutual destruction, or of struggle for political-military supremacy, or of achievement of economic advantage. It is deeply rooted in human sentiment.

It is therefore fitting that the peaceful reunification of Korea should provide humankind with an inspiring example of the Revolution of Peace in the process of nonviolent global transformation.

## NOTES

1. The French Revolution, of course, is to be credited with all three aspirations—*liberté*, *égalité*, and *fraternité*.

2. Transcribed from Eisenhower (1961).

3. Excerpt from a speech before the American Society of Newspaper Editors, April 16, 1953, published dramatically as a full-page advertisement in *The Wall Street Journal* (May 30, 1985: 29), and in other major newspapers. (The advertisement was placed by Joan B. Kroc, widow of Ray Kroc, founder of the McDonald's Corporation, a fast-food restaurant chain.) Eisenhower's imagery of the "cross of iron," of course, is reminiscent of one of the most famous speeches in American political history, the "Cross of Gold" speech in 1896 of Democratic presidential candidate William Jennings Bryan (Koenig, 1971: 197): "You shall not press down upon the brow of labor this cross of thorns, you shall not crucify mankind on a cross of gold."

4. From a British Broadcasting Corporation television interview, August 31, 1958, with Harold Macmillan, quoted in Dennis and Preston (1976: 132).

5. For a recent global survey, see Amnesty International (1987).

6. The report calls for ten priorities in research: "depletion of tropical forests, reduction of biological diversity, cryptic spread of mutant genes, droughts and floods, acid deposition, CO buildup and climate change, impact of hazardous substances on ecosystems and man, loss of productive land due to salinization, impact of urbanization, and meeting current and future energy needs."

7. For an argument that enhanced appreciation of creativity in politics is a major insight to be drawn from the divided Korean experience, see Paige (1965, 1970).

8. For this insight, I am indebted to independent but mutually confirming personal instruction by the distinguished Korean historical scholars Ham Sok Hon in Seoul and by Pak Si Hon in Pyongyang.

9. A suggestion for an institutional response to this need is contained in Paige (1985).

10. This document calls for the abolition of nuclear weapons, the abolition

of bio-chemical weapons and other weapons of mass destruction, the reduction of armed forces to reasonable levels for territorial defense, and the shift of resources saved by the foregoing measures to serve human needs in both rich and poor countries.

11. Some suggestions are made in Paige (1985).

12. Death penalty abolished: Argentina, Austria, Brazil, Canada, Colombia, Costa Rica, Denmark, Dominican Republic, Ecuador, Fiji, Finland, Federal Republic of Germany, France, Greece, Iceland, Italy, Luxembourg, Mexico, Netherlands, New Zealand, Norway, Panama, Papua New Guinea, Portugal, Spain, Sweden, Uruguay, and Venezuela (Amnesty International, 1979: 221–227; Humana, 1987).

13. Conscientious objection to military service permitted: Austria, Australia, Belgium, Boliva, Brazil, Canada, Denmark, Federal Republic of Germany, Finland, France, German Democratic Republic, Guyana, Israel, Italy, Lebanon, Mexico, Netherlands, New Zealand, Norway, Paraguay, South Africa (Whites only), Sweden, Switzerland, Trinidad and Tobago, United Kingdom, United States of America, Uruguay, and Zaire (Kidron and Segal, 1981: map 30).

## REFERENCES

Ambio. (1983). "Environmental Research and Management Priorities for the 1980's," *Ambio: A Journal of the Human Environment*, 12 (2), entire issue.

Amnesty International. (1979). *The Death Penalty*. London: Amnesty International.

———. (1987). *Amnesty International, 1987, Report*. London: Amnesty International.

Burton, John. (1979). *Deviance, Terrorism and War*. New York: St. Martin's.

Dennis, Peter, and Preston, Adrian, eds. (1976). *Soldiers as Statesmen*. New York: Barnes & Noble.

Eisenhower, Dwight David. (1961). "Farewell Broadcast, January 17, 1961," *The Spoken Word* (SW–9403) [sound recording].

Humana, Charles. (1987). *World Human Rights Guide*. London: Pan.

International Foundation for Development Alternatives. (1981). "Manifesto of Nobel Prize Winners," *IFDA Dossier* (September-October): 1(61)–3(63).

Keyes, Gene. (1982). "Force Without Firepower: A Doctrine of Unarmed Military Service," *CoEvolution Quarterly*, 34 (Summer): 4–25.

Kidron, Michael, and Segal, Ronald. (1981). *The State of the World Atlas*. New York: Simon & Schuster.

Koenig, Louis W. (1971). *Bryan*. New York: Putnam's Sons.

Paige, Glenn D. (1965). "Some Implications for Political Science of the Comparative Politics of Korea," *International Conference on the Problems of Modernization in Asia (June 28–July 7, 1965) Report*. Seoul: Korea University, Asiatic Research Center: 388–405. Reprinted in Fred Riggs, ed., *Frontiers of Development Administration*, pp. 139–70. Durham, NC: Duke University Press, 1970.

———. (1980). "Nonviolent Political Science," *Social Alternatives* (Brisbane), 1 (June): 104–12.

———. (1984). "Nonviolent Cultural Resources for Korean Reunification." In Sung-joo Han, ed., *Korea and Asia*, pp. 227–50. Seoul: Korea University Press. Essay written in honor of the sixtieth birthday of Professor Kim Jun-Yop.

———. (1985). "Transnational Consortium for Study of Korean Reunification: A Nonviolent Proposal," paper prepared for the International Symposium on the Reunification of Korea and Peace in Asia, sponsored by the Asian-Pacific Peace Policy Institute, Yokohama International Hall, Japan, July 6–8.

Plimak, E. G., and Karyakin, Yu.F. (1979). "Lenin o mirnoi i nemirnoi formakh revolyutsionnogo perekhoda v sotsializmu" [Lenin on Peaceful and Nonpeaceful Forms of Revolutionary Transition to Socialism], paper presented at the eleventh World Congress of the International Political Science Association, Moscow, August 12–18.

Sharp, Gene. (1973). *The Politics of Nonviolent Action.* Boston: Porter Sargent.

United Nations, General Assembly. (1948). *Universal Declaration of Human Rights.* New York: United Nations. Adopted December 10, 1948.

———. (1978). *Final Document of Assembly Session on Disarmament, 23 May–1 July 1978* (S–10/2). New York: UN Office of Public Information.

———. (1982). *World Charter for Nature* (Resolution 37/7). New York: United Nations. Adopted October 28, 1982.

Zhang Yiping. (1982). "Due feibaoli zhuyi ying jiben kending," [We Should Positively Affirm Nonviolence] *Shijie lishi* [World History], 16 (June 7): 78–80.

# 5     The Mediation Approach to Korean Reunification
## Theodore L. Becker

## THE PROBLEM

All around planet Earth, there are dangerous "flashpoints," political situations capable, under certain circumstances, of triggering a small flashfire that can escalate into nuclear exchanges.

### Korea Divided: A Perennial Danger

The most prominent and explosive of these places currently is the Middle East, where three hostile power blocs are in close contact and interaction and where material and ideological stakes are very high. Another highly combustible flashpoint is the Korean peninsula, which has been a hotspot of tension for several generations.

It is a major priority for the future of humankind to find ways to decrease the chance that hostilities would erupt in any major tinderzone around the world. Thus, many people have tried to calm things down by writing, talking, and interceding in different ways. Unfortunately, most of these attempts by well-intentioned third parties ("peacemakers") have ended mostly in failure: in the Middle East, in Central America, in Northern Ireland, between China and Taiwan, and between South and North Korea.

On the other hand, there have been a few occasional success stories. Most notably, there was the Camp David Accords, where a sustained and determined effort by President Carter of the United States resulted in a mediated agreement between Egypt and Israel. The Arias Peace Plan is an ongoing effort by several neutral but interested South and Central American nations to negotiate and monitor a regional peace plan in Central America, with particular regard to El Salvador and Nicaragua.

The status quo in Korea, between the two Koreas, remains relatively taut and inflammable. This is not good for the world, nor is it good for South Korea or North Korea.

It is true that South Korea has amazed the world by its incredible economic progress over the past two decades. Now it may be on the verge of yet another miracle, a political one, where a modern Asian democracy may emerge from a series of autocratic administrations. All this has been accomplished despite a severe handicap: South Korea is split apart from its Northern region, rich in some natural resources, the dwelling place of one-third of the Korean people.

It is sad, but equally true, that prospects for a comprehensive national reconciliation and/or reunification are not very likely for a long, long time. Deep mistrust and hatred remain the chief legacy of the North Korean invasion of the South in the early 1950s. Bad blood, plots and schemes, and harsh invective characterize the relations between the two Koreas to this very day. No one seriously argues that South Korea would be better off if it would unite with its Northern brothers and sisters. And there is scant opportunity for the North to forge a reunion by force. Thus, the divorce seems permanent right now.

## Negative Consequences for North and South Korea

This rift has heavy consequences for North Korea. The self-styled People's Democracy of Korea is one of the longest running one-man dictatorships in the world. Its economy is, to say the least, underdeveloped and suffers badly in some comparisons with the economic miracle in South Korea (Republic of Korea, 1986b). Its government is increasingly isolated. Its system makes it one of the great underachieving societies in modern times.

Its failures are dramatized by the success of its Southern neighbor. Clearly, the Republic of Korea has much to crow about: a gleaming, modern capital and one of the largest and growing cities anywhere on the face of the earth; a robust and expanding national economy; turbulent politics striving toward democracy; Seoul being selected as the primary host city for the 1988 Summer Olympic Games; etc.

Nevertheless, the high degree of rancor and suspicion between the two Koreas also has negative impacts on the South Korean system as well as on the rest of the world.

Think of it this way: Two neighbors, one rich and one poor, live next door to one another. They despise and distrust each other. In the past, one physically attacked the other and almost overran his property. The other retaliated. Now, each strings barbed wire along the border of their two houses. Each insults the other whenever possible. Each speaks only the worst about the other to their friends. Each worries that the other will try to injure members of their families. They walk around with heavy weapons on their backs and ammunition slung around their shoulders. One even continues to countenance an occasional violent episode against the other.

Does this seem like a happy life, one of contentment? Doesn't this life-style impair the mental and emotional well-being of *both* neighbors? Doesn't this way of life put a tremendous burden on *both* their budgets? A siege mentality is not much fun: it causes stress and strain that disturbs one's physical and psychological equilibrium.

In addition, living under such conditions usually makes the people in each household more difficult to live with. Tension creates anger, leads to interpersonal troubles, erodes the degree of freedom to do what people want to do for fear of relaxing their guard, and causes episodic outbursts of violence.

R. J. Rummel argues that a strong correlation exists between the degrees of freedom in a nation and the likelihood of that country waging war (Rummel, 1984: 277–79). In Rummel's view, nations with a high level of democracy and individual freedom are far less likely to go to war than nations that are tyrannical and curtail individual freedoms. (For a critique of this view, see Vincent, 1987). Nevertheless, by maintaining a high degree of external tension with close neighbors, chances of war increase, the quality of life of each party to that dispute decreases (including degrees of individual freedom), and there is some correlation between the two.

This is not to imply that the two Koreas must aim at a full reconciliation to lessen (or eliminate) the probability of major conflict. Much can be gained economically, socially, and politically through a *broad-gauged* and *systematic* effort to reduce the level of tension and hostility.

Even such a modest effort at conflict resolution cannot be accomplished easily or quickly. But it should be commenced as quickly as possible, albeit with forethought and planning. Some periods of time are more hospitable to moving toward peacefulness than others. We are presently living in the early stages of such an era.

This chapter will discuss and analyze the convergence of several current factors that have created a window of opportunity to improve the relations between the two Koreas, thereby lessening the chances of a Korean flash war that could endanger the planet, and improving the internal conditions of liberty and prosperity for the South Korean people.

These factors include: (1) dramatic, new political developments around the world, particularly involving the Soviet Union, China, and the United States; and (2) major advances in the theory, knowledge, and practice in the field of conflict resolution. Combined with the new democratic movement and the upswing in the technological level of the Republic of Korea, the time appears to be ideal to conceive and implement a new strategy for lessening (not resolving) the dangerous hostilities between the two Koreas.

## IMPORTANT EXTERNAL POLITICAL DEVELOPMENTS

The source of most of the major conflict around the world continues to be the super-conflict between two superpowers, the United States and the Soviet Union. The "cold war" between these two protagonists has pervaded the globe since the end of World War II, dominating the political lives of people on all continents, threatening the very survival of billions of men and women everywhere. Wars, rebellions, coups, strife, and unrest are fed and supported by the two superpowers as they maintain an ideological and strategic struggle for geopolitical supremacy and/or hegemony.

The division of Korea was a direct result of the battle between these two gigantic nations and their philosophies. The Korean War also brought China into the drama as a major player. Thus, it seems safe to say that the continuing dispute between North and South Korea is still largely a function of major, competing external forces.

This does not mean that should a miracle occur, that is, that the U.S. and USSR suddenly agree to be friends and allies, that the two Koreas would just as suddenly reunite and become one again. Forty-plus years of bitterness and killing would take substantial time to overcome. What this does mean is that, depending on the status of the general relationships within and between superpowers, Korea is freer to deal with its own relations at certain times in history than at other times.

There have been several major developments in the 1980s that provide the Korean people with some psychological, social, and political room to reconsider their situation on their own, with less pressure from the outside world and to take some actions accordingly.

## SOVIET UNION, GORBACHEV, *PERESTROIKA*, AND *GLASNOST*

In the Soviet Union, a new type of leader ascended to the top rung of the Communist Party's politburo. What first became obvious was his different style: slick, Westernized, relatively good-humored, adroit at public relations. Style is not substance, but the conceptualization and practice of *glasnost*—or open publicity—in modern Soviet society is more than superficial. This, plus the concept and practice of *perestroika* goes to the heart of attitudes throughout the Party and governmental, economic, and social structures and institutional arrangements in the modern Soviet Union (Gorbachev, 1987.)

Clearly, one major reason for this development is that some very powerful members of the ruling elite came to believe that major systemic alterations were necessary to modernize and make the Soviet economy more efficient and more competitive with the West in the production of consumer goods; provide more intellectual space to encourage technological innovation; and to keep the Party in the vanguard of new social and political thought and action. This has led to unparalleled political-economic experimentation since Lenin's New Economic Policy, even including some first attempts at free(er) elections in the selection of certain local Communist Party officials.

The early policy consequences of these structural and attitudinal shifts are a mixed bag. On the positive side, the Soviet Army began to withdraw from Afghanistan in 1988. Openness, however, still precludes serious critiques of Marxist-Leninism (much like the U.S. media and mainstream political process totally ignore any hard-core Marxist critiques of U.S. capitalism).

Moreover, there is no guarantee that this new liberalization in the USSR will last forever or even for long. Suffice it to say at this point, that it is a major thaw in the "cold war" pattern, one that has enormous potential as long as it lasts to permit experimentation by the Korean people with novel ways to reduce tension and hostilities among themselves.

### Post-Maoist China

Similarly, the Chinese Communist Party, under the post-Maoist leadership of Deng Xiaoping, has embarked upon major structural changes in its political economy and its relationships to the capitalist West. The firm grip of orthodox Maoism has been eased enough to allow, even encourage, a new spirit of free enterprise and entrepreneurialism among the Chinese population.

Both in the Soviet Union and China, the dogma concerning the primacy of strong central planning and control of all aspects of the economic system is being rethought and reworked to open a path for free market forces to channel production. Individual, personal profit and wage incentives are enriching socialist theory as well as increasing many citizens' private wealth. The Chinese government has even established what they call "free enterprise zones," inviting Western capitalists to be partners in a variety of industrial and commercial efforts.

Of course, even casual observers of recent Chinese history are aware that it has been characterized by drastic political swings in relatively short time spans. One can only guess how long the ruling Chinese elite will continue to chart their future in the direction of the "four modernizations."

Also, the Chinese experiment of injecting some capitalist and free enterprise ideas into their economic ideology seems to bar the extension of such "bourgeois liberalization" into the political sphere. Thus, those in the Party who condoned the 1986–87 student protests for more "democracy" fell out of grace and the Party seems to be, at the time of this writing, wary of true democratic discourse at the top of its hierarchy and opposed to any emanating from below.

Nevertheless, as in the Soviet case, it would seem that the present direction and style of the Chinese ruling caste also affords some opportunity for steps to be taken by the Korean people to ameliorate their differences. According to Rummel: "The direction of the Sino-South Korean relationship in the late 1970s and early 80s has been toward detente: indirect trade has sharply increased and a number of recent events in Sino-South Korean relations clearly show a warming trend is underway. In effect, a new status quo is being created that involves the maintenance of peace and stability in Korea" (Rummel, 1987: 47). Also, it would appear that this "new status quo" would have a spillover effect on the North Korean government and its attitudes, sooner or later.

## U.S. TRANSFORMATIONALISM

America in the 1980s is widely believed to be in a decade shaped by the thought, action, and inaction of President Ronald Reagan. His stridently "conservative" rhetoric (calling the USSR "the evil empire"); the blossoming of a secret alliance between the CIA and private, right-wing elements to wage a network of not-too-covert wars around the world; and his support for an extraordinary military buildup would seem to be movements in the opposite direction from those described above.

Most directly related to Asia, however, the Reagan administration eventually altered its course by strongly endorsing and actively backing those opposed to non-Communist authoritarianism. In the Philippines, President Reagan ultimately withdrew his blessing from the Marcos dictatorship to insure a peaceful transition to a more democratic administration. In South Korea, the Reagan administration made it plain to the ruling party in 1987 that it would not support the imposition of martial law to block major, pro-democratic constitutional reform.

More important than Ronald Reagan's policies is the development of what some call the Transformational movement in the United States. This does not attract the kind of media attention as does politics radiating from Washington, D.C., but it is widespread and deep-rooted throughout the United States and it could have tremendous implications for what may or may not happen in Korea.

For example, there have been a number of U.S. analysts and observers who have pointed out that the United States is moving into a new, post-industrial, information age. This has been called by a variety of names including "the Third Wave" (Toffler, 1980), "the Aquarian Conspiracy" (Ferguson, 1981), "the New Age" (Satin, 1979), etc. Its components include antipatriarchal values (feminism); pro-consumerism; the environmental movement; grass-roots democratic developments; the self-improvement and human potential movements; and what might be termed the peace and peacemaking movements.

This loose-knit, but active group of socioeconomic-political organizations and developments is not a political party and they do not work together in any coordinated way. Indeed, they are extremely decentralized and usually operate at the state and local levels. This fits into the general rules of contemporary U.S. politics where national political parties are weak and where many of those who seek radical change in the system and policies of the U.S. industrial, corporate adhere to the maxim: "think globally; act locally."

Their track record, however, is impressive. Looking at the results of various campaigns against large, centralized interests, we find legislation, court action, and citizen initiatives to improve the quality of the air, water, and ground; a slowdown in the development of nuclear energy; increased employment of women and minorities; increased scrutiny of the food supply; etc. In the past few years, there has also been a tremendous amount of growth in the academic field of peace research and in the theory and practice of the ancient art of peacemaking.

Finally, despite the generally negative relations between the U.S. and USSR during Ronald Reagan's tenure of office, the Reagan administration continued the thaw between the United States and China and signed the INF Treaty in 1987 (that eliminated a certain class of intermediate range nuclear missiles). More importantly, there have been key steps taken to construct a new kind of "media-ation" of the nuclear stalemate between the two superpowers. Using new communications technologies and ideas that emanate from the new conflict-resolution movement, "space-bridges" are being built between the Soviet Union and the United States to create electronic dialogues designed to clear

up misunderstandings, exchange information, develop mutual understanding, and discuss future plans for joint projects (Becker, 1987).

## THE PEACEMAKING MOVEMENT: NEW
## APPROACHES IN CONFLICT RESOLUTION

Just as many of the most significant advances in the general U.S.
Transformational movement are being made in small-scale arenas
(state and local), so have major developments in the theory, processes,
and techniques of conflict resolution been the result of work and experimentation at the least visible unit of conflict: the interpersonal
dispute, that is, friction or physical hostilities between two people.

### Lessons from the Interpersonal Mediation Movement

The United States is an incredibly rich laboratory in which to study
all kinds of conflict among all kinds of people using a cornucopia of
conflict-resolution options. The U.S. is well-known to lead the universe
in the number of lawyers per citizen (there are now approximately
750,000 practicing attorneys) and utilizing the adversarial-oriented
law courts to settle controversies seems to be an American obsession.

*Citizen Mediation.*[1] Yet, since the mid-late 1970s, there has been a
dramatic growth in finding other, less confrontational ways to resolve
disputes. This has been, in part, due to the high costs (financial and
personal) of the legal system and in part due to its impenetrability to
most Americans. But it was also originated by a number of scholars,
theorists, and practitioners who believe that dispute resolution in the
U.S. was monopolized by professionals and bureaucracies, a social
structure that along with other similar economic and political structures was largely responsible for widespread alienation, frustration,
tension, and general malaise in the United States.

Thus, the new American mediation movement was strongly characterized at its inception by a desire to find novel ways to manage and
resolve conflict, ways that were rooted in grass-roots neighborhoods
and communities and that were the domain and property of ordinary
citizens (Becker, 1986). This is why most mediation programs are called
"neighborhood justice centers" in the U.S. There was a strong bias
toward citizen participation and the center being situated in local
neighborhoods (McGillis and Mullen, 1977).

Unfortunately, as had been predicted by many observers, the new
American Mediation movement has come to be dominated in many
ways by professionals and bureaucrats of all kinds (Auerbach, 1983).
Instead of being a transformational spearhead in the field of dispute
resolution, it has often turned out to be just another part of the problem
(Becker, 1986). Yet, there are still enough examples, albeit exceptions

to the rule, that neighborhood and community-run and operated programs can be extremely successful on their own terms (Shonholtz, 1984).

For example, there is ample evidence that ordinary citizens, that is, nonprofessional mediators with no special substantive knowledge, can be excellent third party neutrals because of their "creative potential" and their ability to "humanize institutions" (Warhaftig, 1984). Indeed, it is this writer's view that (1) empathy; (2) good listening habits and skills; (3) and near-to-total ignorance of the subject of the dispute are the *best* combination of traits for superior third party intermediaries. This is because these qualities best facilitate open communication between parties firmly entrenched in positions hardened by years of bickering and ill-will.

*Communication as a Step Toward Resolution.* One of the problems with mediation programs that are sponsored and/or funded by large organizations (courts, foundations, bar associations, etc.) is that they focus on the measurable results of the process, that is, cost-benefit analysis (how many cases were handled and how much money was expended; what percentage of the cases that were mediated reached an agreement; does the diversion to mediation significantly reduce the case loads in the court system; and the like [Roehl and Cook, 1985]). This puts a premium on *quantifiable* "success."

On the other hand, this is an excellent example of putting the cart before the horse. It confuses the superficial for the real. It exalts manifest, quick *settlement* of disputes at the expense of the slower, step-by-step successful *resolution* of conflict. The latter depends on increased and improved communication about the root causes of the conflict; about what each party really wants and *needs* to end the problem; and on a creative exploration of new ways to end the dispute.

Mediators of interpersonal disputes have discovered that just getting parties to sign an agreement to a settlement frequently doesn't end the fighting, that is, the accord erodes or collapses thereafter. Yet, sometimes when the parties fail to come to a truly enforceable agreement, the communications processes that were started during the mediation process lead to a general lessening of tension between the disputants and, occasionally, toward eventually resolving the problem to their mutual satisfaction (Felstiner and Williams, 1978).

*Peace and Harmony Over Justice and Truth.* One of the tenets of the new peacemaking movement is that obtaining a satisfactory state of peace and harmony is superior to trying to win what one believes to be justice or trying to prove what is true. In almost all cases of violence, whether involving individuals or nations, each side believes he/she/ they are right and the other side is wrong. Each believes the use of force or violence (whether physical or symbolic) will create a just result. (Is God always on the side of the winner?)

Mediators, being trained and reinforced in the effectiveness of compassionate listening, are struck by the fact that in almost every dispute each party thinks they are absolutely right and the other is absolutely wrong. Each focuses on how good they are and how bad the other is. But if the mediator looks at it from each side's point of view, he or she can easily see how each side believes he/she/it is righteous and the other is evil incarnate.

It is the job of the neutral, third party peacemaker to try to convince each side that truth and justice are relative and illusory, hard to define and slippery to grasp. It is the job of the mediator to help the parties see that continued fighting to achieve what they believe to be justice will result in heavy costs and negative responses even if they "win." In most cases, however, achieving peace and harmony are within reach only if each side really desires it, whether they truly understand the genuine value for themselves in achieving it, that is, the security, serenity, and freedom that peace and harmony inexorably produce.

*Focusing on the Future, Not the Past.* Those who seek to redress wrongs and to establish the truth are often locked into the past. Thus, the legal system is a perfect battlefield for many, since courts and lawyers (surely in the Anglo-American common law system) are bound by precedent in their determinations of what actually happened and who is right. Some international disputes also are fueled—wholly or in part—by strong feelings about who did what to whom in the past, even the recent past. This helps trap parties into positions on issues that are set in concrete. And as long as the disputants continue to dwell in history, even recent history, they are unlikely to change their steadfast positions.

Some futurists see the ancient practice of mediation as having great application for tomorrow and all mediators are practicing futurists (Dator, 1981). They try mightily to get parties to downplay (or even overlook) what happened in the dim and distant time of yesteryear— or even yesterday. There is much in Eastern and Western philosophy and theology that teaches us that bad deeds exact heavy burdens on malefactors and tortfeasors both in this life and any life that transcends our brief sojourns on earth. Carrying the bulging baggage of past wrongs puts a heavy weight on the shoulders of those who want to move into the future.

In successful mediations, parties somehow come to feel that certain things will suffice to bury the past and let them enter the future less burdened. For example, after a successful mediation, parties find that sincere apologies and regrets are somewhat healing. They are willing to negotiate compromises over positions that at one time seemed firm. They are willing to accept promises and plans for future behavior between them that they believe they can live with. And realizing that

mediation has helped them communicate and overcome seemingly irreconcilable differences, they are willing to mediate the future problems and disagreements that may well arise between them again.

*Where Mediation Works Best and Worst.* Of course, mediation and
other third party conflict-resolution methods are not foolproof panaceas
for all disputes. All mediations are not successful and some kinds of
situations are not well-suited for mediation.

For example, many crimes committed by strangers are not good
candidates for mediation. If someone I didn't know shot me at random
on the street, there is not much for me to negotiate about later on. If
I survived, I'd probably want vengeance and would want to help the
state prosecute my assailant to ensure incarceration for a long, long
time.

But what if my brother-in-law battered me because he erroneously
thought I was having an extramarital affair and cheating on his sister?
Should I and the state treat this situation just as if I was assaulted by
a total stranger? Why didn't my brother-in-law discuss the matter with
me? Was there something about our relationship that was an underlying factor in the incident? What effect on my marriage and our family
would such a public prosecution have?

Several years of intensive experience in the new citizens mediation
movement in the U.S. have demonstrated that *mediation works particularly well in ongoing, continuing relationships.* Thus, in disputes
within families, between neighbors, among co-workers, colleagues, and
business partners, etc., there is much to be gained by trying to resolve
the conflict peacefully and amicably than by continuing to struggle for
supremacy, justice, vengeance, or whatever.

The same experience has questioned the general belief that mediation (and other methods of conciliation) works poorest in situations
where one party or side to the dispute has a tremendous material or
psychological power advantage over the other side. Although there is
little systematic research on this proposition, at least one study indi-
cates that disparity in psychological power had little effect on the
outcome of divorce mediations (Thoennis and Pearson, 1985). Thus,
when an individual (particularly one lacking in resources) is pitted
against a large corporation or against the state, it is difficult, but not
impossible, for the third party to help the one in the ostensibly stronger
position see any reason to change his/her/its position.

## From Interpersonal to International

Many experts in international relations, diplomacy, and world affairs
find the lessons and experiences gained in the practice and study of
interpersonal conflict resolution to be of little professional (and/or prac-

tical) interest to them. After all, they say, an international dispute has a much different scale and dynamic than a tiff between a husband and wife. This remains the conventional wisdom, but cracks are beginning to appear in this wall of resistance to change.

There has been an increasing acceptance, for example, of the principles and processes of domestic environmental mediation into international arenas of conflict, in particular to help resolve international environmental disputes. "Environmental mediation offers a form of authority based on consent and voluntary compliance. As such, it is ideally suited to the highly decentralized international system" (Dryzek and Hunter, 1987: 99). This same reasoning also applies to applying the principles of interpersonal mediation to the international sphere.

Nevertheless, it is normal for people who have labored arduously in a field for a long time to resist, if not resent, advice from newcomers, especially when the beginners are viewed as being ignorant of relevant skills and knowledge. But the fact remains that the new arrivals on this scene have a high rate of success in resolving certain conflicts, while the experts in international conflict resolution have a high rate of failure. What is more, there is some evidence that negotiator experience is unrelated to successful outcomes in negotiations (Carnevale and Pegnetter, 1985).

Of course it is true that the scale of the conflict is different when the struggle is between two nations rather than two individuals, and this variation has important effects. For example, such a disparity in scale is a major intervening variable in the vastly different communications problems that exist in resolving disputes between individuals and nations. We know how two people can communicate with each other in a face-to-face encounter, but how do citizens of two nations communicate with each other?

On the other hand, feelings of anger, hate, rejection, and despair are the same in individuals acting alone as they are in individuals acting as a group or on behalf of a group (nations). Spirals of escalating hostilities exist in both interpersonal and international disputes.

Finally, there are similar obstacles to be surmounted in resolving international, as well as interpersonal, disputes. For example, in both situations, mediators must succeed in (1) persuading two or more enemies or warring factions that they have something important to gain (and less to lose) by diminishing or ending the hostilities; (2) helping them listen to and communicate with each other in more understanding and empathetic ways; (3) helping them seriously construct and consider new ways to end the battle in a mode that is mutually advantageous and/or satisfactory; and (4) helping them learn relevant theories and techniques of conflict resolution so they can nip future conflict in the bud.

Given the enormous amounts of time, energy, and national wealth spent on preparing for war or on national defenses and deterrents, it would appear eminently worthwhile (and much less expensive) to spend substantial time and money on experiments to see if and how lessons learned in the interpersonal mediation movement can be successfully applied in volatile, long-term international disputes. The proof will not come in which theory is more persuasive (the theories and techniques of interpersonal conflict resolution are/are not applicable in international conflict), but whether these new ideas and skills are more effective in helping resolve international disputes than traditional ones.

*New Approaches to International Conflict Resolution.* The field of international conflict resolution—having a high frustration quotient—needs fresh ideas to improve its success ratio. In recent times, there have been several developments worth further exploration and application. The following brief synthesis is meant to be representative, not exhaustive, of these new concepts and limited tests. As a model, I believe they may prove to have use in helping alleviate such protracted, deeply rooted conflicts like that persisting on the Korean peninsula.

Jacob Bercovitch is a New Zealand political scientist interested in international dispute resolution and the role of third parties in helping resolve such conflicts. He has also had personal experience in the interpersonal dispute resolution movement. In a recent book, he devised the theoretical construct in Figure 5.1.

Bercovitch acknowledges and incorporates the theoretical and practical contributions of John Burton in his analysis. Burton, a former diplomat as well as interpersonal and international mediator, has invented a promising approach to third party international conflict resolution (TPICR) that emphasizes the *problem-solving* aspects of the process (see Burton, 1984).

*Second-Track Diplomacy.* The most important addition to the practice of TPICR made by Burton's work is his concept of the "seminar" approach. He classifies this process as *second-track diplomacy*. There are several reasons for this.

In second-track diplomacy, the locus of international conflict resolution shifts from government and/or professional sites to an academic environment. Instead of the major intermediaries being government officials, quasi-governmental officials or governmental surrogates, they are professionals in conflict-resolution processes and people with expertise in substantive fields relevant to resolving the dispute. In second-track diplomacy, private professionals in peacemaking—theorists, scholars, practitioners—assume the major burden of helping warring factions understand more about the dynamics of their conflict, as well as about the process of peacemaking itself.

This new approach emphasizes (1) resolution instead of settlement;

Figure 5.1
Problem-Solving and Third Party Intervention

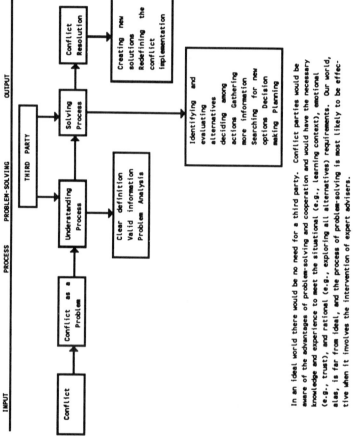

INPUT      PROCESS      PROBLEM-SOLVING      OUTPUT

THIRD PARTY

Conflict → Conflict as a Problem → Understanding Process → Solving Process → Conflict Resolution

Understanding Process: Clear definition / Valid information / Problem Analysis

Solving Process: Identifying and evaluating alternatives deciding among actions Gathering more information Searching for new options Decision making Planning

Conflict Resolution: Creating new solutions Redefining the conflict implementation

In an ideal world there would be no need for a third party. Conflict parties would be aware of the advantages of problem-solving and cooperation and would have the necessary knowledge and experience to meet the situational (e.g., learning context), emotional (e.g., trust), and rational (e.g., exploring all alternatives) requirements. Our world, alas, is far from ideal, and the process of problem-solving is most likely to be effective when it involves the intervention of expert advisers.

Source: Berkovitch (1984: 25).

(2) noncoercive, informational processes; (3) informal, relaxed settings; and (4) private instead of official facilitation. Early indications are that it works, albeit in pilot projects and experimental situations (Burton, 1987). What it needs is abundant support and extensive application.

Second-track diplomatic efforts are being attempted presently in a center at George Mason University in Virginia (where Burton is now located); in the Carter Center at Emory University (Atlanta, Georgia); and at the University of Hawaii's Institute for Peace. The latter intends to limit its services to helping resolve serious and/or long-term conflicts in the Asia-Pacific region.

*Third-Track Conflict Resolution.* Recent work by Becker takes these ideas and practices even further by recognizing that communication processes in international conflict resolution must involve the public(s), even at the earliest stages in important and meaningful ways. This can and must be done even in such mega-conflicts directly pitting the two superpowers against one another, for example, the U.S.-USSR nuclear stalemate (Becker, 1987, 1988). Clearly, public-to-public communication was difficult in bygone days, when methods of TPICR were first implemented. However, with modern communications marvels such as radio, TV, space satellites, telephones, and computers, it is not only feasible, but necessary. This concept might best be labeled *third-track conflict resolution* since it incorporates all aspects of second-track diplomacy, but (1) adds the publics of the disputing nations as parties, and (2) includes professionals in high-tech communications and public opinion as new-mode intermediaries.

It is particularly important to develop third-track conflict resolution because when international conflict erupts into violence, it is the people of the embattled nations who suffer the most. One finds few government officials and professionals in the front lines and foxholes. Also, in interpersonal disputes, the parties themselves are directly and immediately involved in the third party resolution processes. They hear and talk in the presence of their foe or foes. In international disputes, they are *represented* by governmental officials. But there are gaping holes in the communications systems between all governments and all peoples, some larger than others. Thus, in TPICR there needs to be better communication between the representatives of the publics involved and the publics themselves.

One solution to the problem of communication lapses and gaps between the representatives of a public and that public involved in an international dispute is to engage that public through direct democratic processes in discussing and voting on the problem and the various bargaining and negotiating positions and bottom lines. This can be aided and abetted in modern, industrialized nations by "electronic town meetings", or ETMs (see Barber, 1985; Becker and Scarce, 1986; Arterton, 1987). It is important to expose most international dispute negotiations (although not necessarily those involving the highest level military secrets) to the relevant publics (gaining their assent and support) so as to avoid future collapses of hard-earned, apparently workable agreements—as demonstrated recently in Northern Ireland and Sri Lanka, where hard-bargained accords between government officials at the highest levels were rejected by the actual combatants.

The third parties in the third-track process must have similar qualities to mediators and conciliators in interpersonal dispute resolution. They must be neutral and they must be trusted by both (all) parties. In the North-South Korean context, they should be non-official, conflict resolution and media professionals specializing in democratic, interactive processes. Ideally, they should work as a team and come from a variety of countries—some friendly or acceptable to each side so as to insure fairness in the presentation of the facts and arguments. For example, a team of third party facilitators might include experts from (1) the U.S.A.; (2) the Soviet Union and/or China; and (3) New Zealand, Costa Rica, Switzerland, Sweden, etc. Such a panel would be designed to maximize fair and balanced presentations of information and opinion and to encourage open and honest expressions of feelings and sentiments.

All this being said, it is time to fit all these pieces together and try to apply these ideas to the precarious situation presently existing in Korea.

## SOME FAVORABLE CONDITIONS AND KEY PROBLEMS

The present approach or approaches to settling or resolving the enduring conflict or specific flare-ups between the two Koreas seems to be predominantly first-track, traditional two party negotiations with occasional employment of third party go-betweens (some of whom are private and nongovernmental, for example, the Red Cross, the International Olympic Committee, etc.). With the prominent exception of allowing families who were split up by the division of Korea in 1945 to have reunions in 1985, the attempts at Korean conciliation can generally be characterized as classic, piecemeal attempts that center on specific issues and/or positions.

For example, the most recent proposal for North-South Korean negotiations offered by the Republic of Korea states that its goal is to "reduce tension on the Korean peninsula and fulfill the aspiration of the entire Korean people for peaceful reunification through dialogue and negotiation in the spirit of reunification" (Republic of Korea, 1987: 5).

This statement then recites a litany of failed talks on a wide range of subjects (economic, military, athletics). As a solution, it proposes talks between the Foreign Ministers of South and North Korea on a wide range of issues (including a non-aggression agreement) that could be held in New York City, Panmunjom, or wherever agreeable to both parties.

This approach has value, particularly since such talks, if held, would be the first between North and South Korean foreign ministers and, if successful, could even pave the way for talks at the highest level. It has potential for "restoring trust and improving relations between the South and the North." However, this approach, *by itself*, has almost no hope of realizing the other objective iterated by the South Korean government, that is, meeting its "responsibility to reunify the divided country." This is precisely where second- and third-track diplomacy needs to be utilized additionally and, whenever possible, simultaneously.

## South Korean Conditions Favorable to Second- and Third-Tracks

The more open and democratic a society, the more likely that second- and third-track methods of conflict resolution can be seeded, cultivated, and will flourish. These methods are best nurtured by free and independent universities and research centers and by open and independent communications systems available to internal and external entrepreneurs and to the public in general and at large.

Recent political developments in South Korea—particularly if they lead to even more open, democratic processes in the future—are an extremely favorable condition for the use and growth of these new approaches to conflict resolution. The more de jure and de facto democracy, the better. This opens the door to independent, decentralized, and effective experimentation and practice in the art and science of dispute resolution. This will be particularly important for discovering what principles and processes developed in other cultures will work best, or not at all, in the Korean cultural context (Becker and Slaton, 1987).

A more democratic political system will also increase the opportunities for more open and freer discussion and dialogue between the South Korean government and its people and between various factions in the South Korean public itself. Such massive public-government discourse and public-public interaction is feasible in South Korea since it is one of the technological and communications giants of Asia. By way of example, South Korea has an extremely high rate of telephone penetration, reaching "over 70 percent of all households" in the country (Republic of Korea, 1986b: 70). It also ranks very high in television sets and radios per household.

### Key Problems in Using Second- and Third-Tracks in South Korea

A major obstacle standing in the way of any significant progress toward less hostile relations between North and South Korea is the almost total lack of communications between the two governments—and what is even worse—between individual citizens of these two related, but divided, countries. In addition to the deeply felt negative emotions, and despite the revision of the Anti-Communist Laws in 1981, there remain laws and customs that forbid certain personal contacts, oral or written discussion, or exchanges of ideas between the citizens of the two Koreas. There is no public mail or telephone exchange system. North Korean books are not sold in the South.

In order to even begin to apply the lessons learned in successful interpersonal mediation (particularly: "communication as a step toward resolution" and "focus on the future, not the past") at least one of the feuding parties *must* take the first step toward a more open communications process between the two. For example, a systematized, ever-increasing variety of exchanges could be planned and offered: cultural, educational, scientific, athletic, and economic. Some of these might be conducted via teleconferences or computer conferences, some televised nationally. Even though occasional past efforts along these lines may not have been successful, a steadily increasing set of offers under present and future external political conditions has an excellent chance of bearing fruit.

In some crucial ways, South Korea seems to be in a strong enough position to adopt such a future conflict resolution strategy since it has an able, well-equipped military security system, a powerful and reliable ally (the United States), superior communications technology, and what promises to be a much freer, democratic system.

If the South Korean society moved in such a direction, what guarantee would there be that such a strategy would positively impact the North Korean government? Since North Korea is a highly controlled society, is there any hope that any of this would get through to the people there or that it would make a positive impression on them? Might it not, instead, be seen as a sign of weakness that could multiply the number and range of demands made by the North Korean government? What if one side is willing to enter second- and third-track TPICR but the other is not? What if one side is open to communication but the other is not? What if one side continues to be violent while the other is not?

The past, present, and future situation between the People's Republic of China (PRC) and the government of Taiwan may provide a useful analogy. Much the same enmity and lack of relations and communication exists between these two countries as between North and South Korea. In similar fashion, each side has prohibited its citizens from traveling to the other country. However, in 1979 the PRC (either for propaganda purposes or as an early sign of what was to come) offered direct links with Taiwan in transportation, trade, and postal service. Taiwan refused.

Now, due in large part to the changing political situations discussed earlier in this essay, Taiwan has decided to permit private Taiwan citizens to visit the mainland and to allow elderly Chinese citizens to visit Taiwan. According to Taiwanese Premier Yu Kuo-Hwa: "We are now ready to launch an offensive, not of weapons, but of something much more powerful—ideas."

Increasing the channels of communication within South Korea and between the two Koreas would probably produce an asymmetrical situation at first. North Korea would tend to react negatively and/or in ways that might be frustrating. However, as in interpersonal conflict situations, this would still put internal and external pressures on the North Korean government to eventually accept these new conditions sooner or later. An illustration of external pressure would be any continued relaxation of communication barriers between the PRC and Taiwan, or continued warming relations between the PRC and South Korea. Once processes of increased communications and effective conflict resolution get started, they gain a momentum that is hard to resist.

## CONCLUSION

Third party dispute resolution processes have a magic in them, a quality to help transform conflict into peace—under certain conditions.

It seems that very extraordinary political events are converging in a way that provides ample room to develop and test new ways to turn down the heat in several nuclear flashpoints around the world and, consequently, free up resources to solve major economical and ecological problems.

In particular, the enduring precipitous situation between the two Koreas presents a rare opportunity for the growth of innovative and useful tools in international conflict resolution. The external political factors are right; there is a huge potential for more and stronger democracy in South Korea; South Korea is relatively secure militarily and economically; and the hardware and software for implementing second- and third-track conflict resolution is readily adaptable to the Korean cultural context.

Two useful steps to be taken in planning and executing a future conflict-resolution strategy for the Korean situation, would seem to be: (1) the development of a major Korean peacemaking and conflict-resolution "growth industry"—first- , second- , and third-tracks and (2) the effective nonenforcement of most, if not all, the laws and mores that limit communication about the North-South division, between South and North Korea, and between South Korean citizens.

The famous British pop singer, John Lennon, once sang "give peace a chance." Peace is too important to be left to chance. It needs commitment. People and nations that seek peace from conflict need to make such a commitment and take some risks. They must continually strive for a freer and more democratic society at home, maintain adequate strength to deter aggression against their homeland, and constantly seek new ways to resolve conflict with those who threaten them most.

## NOTES

I would like to thank several fellow political scientists for their excellent constructive critiques of this essay, all of which helped improve it immensely: Dr. Chung Tuk-Chu (Soongsil University); Dr. Suh Dae-Sook (University of Hawaii at Manoa); Dr. Ko Seung-Kyun (Hawaii Loa College); and last, but certainly not least, Dr. R. J. Rummel (University of Hawaii at Manoa). I, of course, take full responsibility for the contents.

1. I am using the term "mediation" generically to include various methods of third party conflict management and/or dispute resolution, but most particularly that which is termed "conciliation."

## REFERENCES

Arterton, F. Christopher. (1987). *Teledemocracy*. Beverly Hills, CA: Sage.

Auerbach, Gerald. (1983). *Justice Without Law?* New York: Oxford University Press.

Barber, Benjamin. (1985). *Strong Democracy*. Berkeley: University of California Press.

Becker, Ted. (1986). "Paradox in the New American Mediation Movement: Status Quo and Social Transformation," *Missouri Journal of Dispute Resolution*: 109–29.

———. (1987). *Mediating the Nuclear Stalemate*. Santa Barbara, CA: Nuclear Age Peace Foundation.

———. (1988). "Mediating and Media-ating the Nuclear Stalemate." In David Krieger, ed., *Waging Peace in the Nuclear Age*. Santa Barbara, CA: Capra Publishing.

Becker, Ted, and Scarce, Richard (1986). "Teledemocracy Emergent." In

Brenda Dervin and Melvin Voigt, eds., *Progress in Communication Science*, vol. 9, pp. 263–86. Norwood, NJ: Ablex Publishing.

Becker, Ted, and Slaton, Christa Daryl. (1987). "Cross-Cultural Mediation Training," *Mediation Quarterly*, 18 (Fall): 55–66.

Bercovitch, Jacob. (1984). *Social Conflicts and Third Parties: Strategies of Conflict Resolution*. Boulder, CO: Westview.

Burton, John. (1984). *Global Conflict: The Domestic Sources of International Conflict*. College Park, MD: Center for International Development.

———. (1987). *Resolving Deep-Rooted Conflict: A Handbook*. Lanham, MD: University Press of America.

Carnevale, P., and Pegnetter, R. (1985). "The Selection of Mediation Tactics in Public Sector Disputes," *Journal of Social Issues*, 41 (2): 65–81.

Dator, James A. (1981). "Inventing a Judiciary for the State of Ponape," *Political Science*, 33 (June): 94–99.

Dryzek, John S., and Hunter, Susan. (1987). "Environmental Mediation for International Problems," *International Studies Quarterly*, 31 (1): 87–102.

Felstiner, W. L. F., and Williams, Lynne A. (1978). "Mediation as an Alternative to Criminal Prosecution: Ideology and Limitations," *Law and Human Behavior*, 2 (3): 223–44.

Ferguson, Marilyn. (1981). *The Aquarian Conspiracy*. Los Angeles: Tarcher.

Gorbachev, Mikhail. (1987). *Perestroika*. New York: Harper & Row.

McGillis, Daniel, and Mullen, Joan. (1977). *Neighborhood Justice Centers*. Washington, DC: U.S. Department of Justice.

Korea, Republic of. (1986b).* *A Comparative Study of the South and North Korean Economies*. Seoul: National Reunification Board.

———. (1987). *New Initiatives for Peace in Korea*. Seoul: Korean Overseas Information Service.

Roehl, J. A., and Cook, R. (1985). "Issues in Mediation: Rhetoric and Reality Revisited," *Journal of Social Issues*, 41 (2): 161–78.

Rummel, R. J. (1984). *In the Minds of Men: Principles Toward Understanding and Waging Peace*. Seoul: Sogang University Press.

———. (1987). "American Troops in Korea and the Potential for War," unpublished manuscript.

Satin, Mark. (1979). *New Age Politics*. New York: Dell.

Shonholtz, Raymond. (1984). "Neighborhood Justice Systems: Work, Structure, and Guiding Principles," *Mediation Quarterly*, 15 (September): 1–24.

Thoennis, N. A., and Pearson, J. (1985). "Predicting Outcomes in Divorce Mediation: The Influence of People and Process," *Journal of Social Issues*, 41 (2): 115–26.

Toffler, Alvin. (1980). *The Third Wave*. New York: Bantam.

Vincent, Jack. (1987). "On Rummel's Omnipresent Theory," *International Studies Quarterly*, 31 (1): 119–25.

Warhaftig, Paul. (1984). "Nonprofessional Conflict Resolution," *Villanova Law Review*, 29 (6): 1,463–474.

*Korea (1986a) is found in the Select Bibliography.

# 6    The Negotiation Approach to Korean Reunification

## Oran R. Young

The Korean peninsula supports a population of well over 50 million people who constitute a single nation by almost any reasonable criterion. The Korean people form a remarkably homogeneous group in ethnic terms; there is no Korean counterpart to the ethnic diversity of countries like Canada, the United States, and India. All Koreans speak the same language, which is quite distinct from other East Asian languages, such as Chinese or Japanese. They share a common heritage of history stretching over several thousand years and encompassing periods of both political and cultural prominence (for example, the period of the Silla dynasty). Despite the impact of the centrifugal forces of the postwar era, moreover, it is hard to deny the continued existence of a distinctive Korean culture throughout the peninsula. Since 1948, on the other hand, the Korean nation has been governed by two distinct states, the Republic of Korea (ROK) in the South and the Democratic People's Republic of Korea (DPRK) in the North. What is more, these states possess fundamentally antagonistic political institutions, have a history of violent opposition to each other's juridical claims, maintain effective barriers to interaction among their citizens, and support socioeconomic systems which now differ sharply from one another. Under the circumstances, it is perfectly understandable that efforts to unify the Korean nation politically constitute a profound concern among Korean leaders as well as members of the Korean public. Yet it is hardly surprising that there has been little progress toward achieving this goal during the last 40 years.

This chapter examines the applicability of theoretical perspectives on social conflict, collective choice, and political integration to the problem of political unification in Korea. It makes no attempt to formulate a specific prediction concerning the likelihood of peaceful unification within a specified time frame. Rather, it assesses the usefulness of the relevant theoretical perspectives in the search for insights relating to Korean unification and draws out certain policy implications of these alternative ways of looking at the problem of peaceful unification in Korea.

## THE DEPENDENT VARIABLE: PEACEFUL UNIFICATION

Before examining various processes through which unification might occur, it will help to clarify the nature of peaceful unification as a dependent variable. Casual commentaries on political unification typically equate unification with the emergence of a unified state (on the model of the United States or even France) operating under a well-defined constitution laying out comprehensive political and legal institutions. For our purposes, however, it is more fruitful to think about unification as a spectrum of conditions differentiated in terms of (1) the extent to which political and legal institutions are articulated formally; (2) the degree of centralization exhibited by these institutions; and (3) the scope of these institutions in functional terms. At one end of this spectrum, we can place unitary states such as France. The other end of the spectrum is anchored by what Deutsch and others (1957) have called pluralistic security communities. These are groupings of two or more political entities (for example, Norway and Sweden) that remain quite distinct except in the sense that they have developed informal institutions governing security issues among themselves. Between these extremes lies a range of intermediate forms of unification. Thus, we can easily identify federal systems (for example, the United States), confederal systems (for example, Canada), and somewhat looser associations that nevertheless go beyond pluralistic security communities (for example, the Germanic confederation of the nineteenth century). A little ingenuity might well suggest additional points of interest along this spectrum.

There is no reason to assume that specific political systems will follow a simple progression along this spectrum, evolving from pluralistic security communities to federal or unitary states over time. While much of the twentieth century was an era of centralization in political terms, this period is now over. In fact, recent years have witnessed a striking rise in pressures for political devolution, even in well-established European states (for example, France and Great Britain). Nor is there any compelling reason to suppose that the emergence of more highly centralized political institutions constitutes a form of progress.

Here, too, the conventional wisdom of earlier years has given way to ambivalence (Levy 1972: esp. 21–25). Pressures to increase centralization to promote administrative efficiency within welfare states are still very much in evidence, but they are now opposed by countervailing forces backing decentralization in the interests of protecting civil liberties and making government sensitive to the needs of the people.

Consider next the distinction between political unification and economic or sociocultural unification. Political unification refers to the existence of a state or at least a recognizable set of political and legal institutions. Socioeconomic unification, by contrast, has to do with the existence of an integrated economic system and the presence of the attributes of nationhood among the inhabitants of a geographical area. Though the primary concern of this essay is political integration, it is worth inquiring about the links between political unification and other forms of unification. Is economic or sociocultural unification a necessary condition for political unification or vice versa? A few simple examples will suffice to demonstrate that there are no necessary links among these several types of unification. The Austro-Hungarian Empire was unified in political terms, but it certainly did not exhibit a high degree of sociocultural or even economic unification. Economic integration has reached a remarkably high level among the members of the European Economic Community in the absence of political unification extending beyond the minimum condition of a security community. Moreover, contemporary Korea itself illustrates the possibility of a relatively high degree of cultural unification occurring in the absence of political unification.

Nonetheless it is apparent that there are significant links between political unification and economic or sociocultural conditions.[1] Political institutions characteristically reflect the deeper societal structure of the communities in which they operate. This becomes important in the case of Korea because the North and the South are drifting apart in economic and sociocultural terms at a comparatively rapid rate. Within another generation, the economic and sociocultural differences between the two segments of the Korean population can be expected to constitute a formidable barrier to political unification, regardless of the interests or desires of political leaders at the time. While the existence of a single Korean nation is not a sufficient condition to bring about political unification at the present time, there can be little doubt that the continued growth of economic and sociocultural divergences will serve as an increasing barrier to political unification with the passage of time.

Turn now to the notion of *peaceful* unification. In this chapter, I shall use the term peaceful to mean nonviolent. Violence, in turn, refers to the physical destruction of life or property.[2] Accordingly, any process leading to political unification in the absence of significant physical destruction of life or property will be included under the rubric of peaceful unification. This means that there is no contradiction between peaceful unification and the use of various forms of coercion on the part of parties interested in the achievement of unification. Accordingly, it will be important in the course of this chapter to compare and contrast coercive and noncoercive processes through which political unification in Korea might occur.

At this point, we are ready to explore these processes in some detail. It is possible to identify several distinct processes through which unified political institutions for the entire Korean peninsula might emerge. Not surprisingly, each of these processes rests on different theoretical underpinnings and suggests different policy implications. The next four sections of this chapter deal with the processes more relevant to the Korea case.

## NEGOTIATED UNIFICATION

In the first instance, the parties may endeavor to reach agreement on a unified political system for the Korean peninsula through some process of negotiation. That is, they may bargain over the terms of a "constitutional" contract laying out political institutions for the peninsula.[3] While there is room for great variation in the substantive provisions of "constitutional" contracts, any such contract would involve explicit consent on the part of the principals as well as formal expression of the terms of their agreement.

The study of negotiation as a route to peaceful unification rests on the following assumptions. The principal parties to any "constitutional" contract would be the Republic of Korea and the Democratic People's Republic of Korea, though other parties might play some role as guarantors. Each of these parties or players can be treated as a purposive decisionmaker capable of expressing preferences among policy alternatives. Neither the ROK nor the DPRK will experience fundamental regime change prior to reaching an agreement on unification. Accordingly, we can assume that the underlying preferences (that is, value systems) of the principal parties are stable. Additionally, the relationship between the parties is characterized by interdependent decisionmaking or strategic interaction. This means that each party will find the outcomes flowing from its own choices significantly affected by the choices of the other party(ies) (Rapoport, 1964: Ch. 4).

These assumptions make it possible to analyze negotiations pertaining to unification in terms of the theory of bargaining.[4] There are two major cases to consider, distributive bargaining and productive bargaining. Distributive bargaining, the subject of most theoretical work

**Figure 6.1**
**Negotiation Payoff Space**

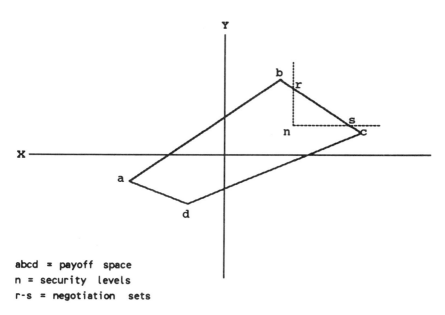

abcd = payoff space
n = security levels
r-s = negotiation sets

on negotiation, becomes the focus of attention whenever the relationship between the parties can be characterized in terms of a fixed payoff space. This will be the case when the parties are in possession of complete information pertaining to the identity of the players participating in a choice problem, the strategies (that is, alternative choices) available to each of the players, and the payoffs associated with each combination of strategy choices on the part of the players. Situations of this sort can be visualized in terms of an Edgeworth box diagram or the well-known graphic formulations of the theory of games (Luce and Raiffa, 1957: Ch. 6). For ease of exposition, let us think in terms of the game-theoretic notion of a payoff space (Figure 6.1).

Now, distributive bargaining refers to the search for agreement on a specific or unique point within the payoff space. Each party is presumed to desire an agreement favoring its own interests to the maximum degree possible. Thus, party X will be motivated to begin by proposing agreement on a point at or near the southeast corner of the payoff space, while party Y will suggest a point at or near the northwest corner of the space. Bargaining itself encompasses all those processes through which the parties converge toward a common or mutually agreeable point in the payoff space. These processes may involve a sequence of offers and counteroffers, the use of various committal tactics, or the identification of what Schelling calls a salient or prominent outcome.[5] In any case, agreement occurs or a bargain is struck when the parties voluntarily accept the same point within the payoff space. We ordinarily assume that this point will be located in the welfare frontier (b-c), simply because there will be alternative agreements benefiting everyone so long as the parties have not reached the welfare frontier (Luce and Raiffa, 1957: Ch. 6). Beyond this, however, there are no restrictions on the agreements reached, so long as they are mutually acceptable to the parties.

A necessary condition for the emergence of an agreement in situations of this type is the existence of a contract zone or a negotiation set (that is, a range of feasible outcomes that both sides would prefer to their security levels or what they can guarantee for themselves by acting in a unilateral or uncoordinated manner).[6] It is this condition that most observers believe cannot be fulfilled in the Korean case at the present time. This is so because both the ROK and the DPRK appear to prefer the status quo (that is, their security levels) to any feasible agreement involving political unification. As Nathan White has put it, each side insists "that the government of a future united Korea be essentially the same as the one currently in existence in their half of the country," and each prefers the status quo to unification on terms perceived as favoring the other side to any significant degree (White, 1978: 351). An obvious implication of this proposition is that it is pointless (except in propaganda terms) for either side to advance elaborate proposals packaged to look like serious offers in a context of distributive bargaining. While such proposals may have certain political attractions either domestically or within the international arena, they can do nothing but make the principal parties suspicious of each other's intentions in the absence of a negotiation set.[7]

Note also that the existence of a negotiation set is not a sufficient condition for success in connection with distributive bargaining. There are several reasons why parties may fail to reach agreement even in the presence of large potential gains from striking a bargain. Thus, the parties may (1) reach a stalemate due to an inability to back away from conflicting commitments; (2) fail to strike a bargain because of the absence of a compensation mechanism suitable for working out side payments; or (3) be unwilling to accept an otherwise suitable agreement out of a fear of cheating or noncompliance when it comes to implementing the bargain (Schelling, 1966: esp. Ch. 2, 5). Under the circumstances, it is important to understand that the mere emergence of a negotiation set is no guarantee of success in distributive bargaining. This is critical in the Korean case since there are good reasons for believing that the problems outlined in this paragraph would loom large even if the difficulty associated with the absence of a negotiation set could somehow be overcome. Once again, therefore, it seems reasonable to conclude that the simple enunciation of new or revised negotiating positions will contribute little toward promoting a process of unification through negotiation in Korea.

Contrast these problems of distributive bargaining with the case of productive bargaining. The basic conditions associated with productive bargaining do not differ from those underlying distributive bargaining. We remain concerned with situations in which purposive parties seek to advance their own interests under conditions of interdependent decisionmaking. But now the parties are no longer in possession of complete information pertaining to the identity of all relevant players, the strategies available to each player, and the payoffs associated with each combination of strategy choices. What this means is that the character of the relationship among the parties is no longer clearcut and may be subject to exercises in reality construction on the part of the parties themselves. Even though they continue to be motivated by the pursuit of their own interests, players faced with situations of this sort may well find it interesting to bargain or negotiate with each other in an exploratory mode, exchanging information in an effort to identify common interests that might serve as a basis for a negotiated settlement (Gross, 1969: Ch. 1).[8] Productive bargaining, therefore, takes the form of a discovery process, the object of which is to improve the information available to the parties concerning the nature of their relationship; it does not involve a series of offers and counteroffers linked to a well-defined negotiation set. Understandably, productive bargaining will often fail. The parties may simply discover that their relationship does not encompass significant common interests. Yet it is by no means uncommon for productive bargaining to uncover substantial common interests that were previously unidentified and that subsequently become bases for successful processes of distributive bargaining.

Productive bargaining may result in any number of alterations in a payoff space tentatively assigned to a situation characterized by interdependent decisionmaking. Specific strategies may be added to or removed from the set of choices available to one or more of the parties.[9] New information may lead to the recomputation of outcomes associated with certain combinations of strategies; this will of course alter the configuration of the payoff space. Similarly, the parties may discover the advantages of package deals, raising the prospects of reaching agreement by joining together issues that were previously handled in separate negotiations. By the same token, they may discover virtues in disaggregating complex problems, negotiating agreements on certain isolable issues as a prelude to tackling other issues during a later time period (Walton and McKersie, 1965: Ch. 5). Further, there are cases in which productive bargaining leads to an expansion of negotiations to include one or more additional parties. A partnership that is mutually advantageous with three or four participants may not work at all with only two principals. Thus, productive bargaining is a much more free-form exercise than distributive bargaining. It is limited only by the imagination of the parties and their willingness to set aside conflicting preferences long enough to engage in a creative search for previously unidentified common interests.

What are the prospects for productive bargaining in the Korean case? Unfortunately, both the ROK and the DPRK are in the habit of treating their relationship as one in which the payoff space is fixed and characterized by the absence of a negotiation set. Accordingly, each side contents itself, for the most part, with the articulation of proposals for unification that are highly repetitive and that cover only a small segment of the range of potential agreements. Should the ROK and the DPRK develop a serious interest in taking steps toward unification on mutually acceptable terms, however, productive bargaining offers some interesting possibilities. To illustrate, the parties might disaggregate the problem, taking concrete steps toward cooperative relations in certain functionally limited areas. Such steps would minimize mutual fears of subversion and cheating.[10] The parties might explore the potential of a consortium of outside powers serving as guarantors of some of the essential features of a scheme for the unification of Korea. A neutralized Korea on the model of Switzerland or Austria, for example, would undoubtedly have considerable appeal in the international arena.[11] Moreover, both the ROK and the DPRK might discover genuine common interests in protecting the Korean peninsula from outside incursions. The geopolitical position as well as the modern history of Korea suggests that this should be a central theme of the politics of the Korean peninsula.

Above all, however, productive bargaining requires a willingness to engage in exploratory negotiations without a predetermined agenda or collection of explicit proposals. The point of productive bargaining at its best is to permit two or more parties to explore each other's underlying concerns and perceptions in an atmosphere that does not pose constant reminders of the conflicts of interest associated with prior expressions of policy. Of course, productive bargaining will not occur at all in the Korean case unless both the ROK and the DPRK develop a genuine interest in reexamining the character of their relationship in a creative fashion. Yet it is at least possible to imagine circumstances that might lead to the emergence of such an interest, even in the absence of fundamental regime change on either side.

## COERCIVE DIPLOMACY

Should bargaining fail or seem too chancy, one or both of the parties may resort to coercion, attempting to force others to accept the unification of Korea on their own terms through measures short of overt violence. The study of coercion as a unification process starts from assumptions that are similar to those underlying the theory of bargaining. We assume a group of actors (now perhaps including outsiders as well as principals) who are capable of purposive behavior and who possess more or less stable preferences. Further, these actors regularly find themselves involved in situations characterized by interdependent decisionmaking. Yet coercive diplomacy differs from ordinary bargaining in several critical respects. There is no search for a mutually beneficial agreement representing a point on a negotiation set. Similarly, there is no convergence process through which the parties narrow their original differences by making a series of offers and counteroffers. The essence of coercion is the effort on the part of the individual player to bring pressure to bear on an adversary, endeavoring to force the adversary to acquiesce to a preferred alternative by making the other alternatives seem unattractive.[12] Not surprisingly, the outcomes flowing from exercises in coercion are less likely to receive formal expression than the results of bargaining, though they may eventually come to be recognized by all parties as binding (Young, 1968: Ch. 12).

It is possible to differentiate several major classes of coercive stratagems which may be applicable to the case of Korean unification. Threats revolve around expressions of intent to inflict harm on an adversary unless the target of the threats conforms to the demands or requirements of the threatener.[13] In this connection, we must distinguish threats, which refer to actions harmful to the threatener as well as the victim, from warnings, which are mere announcements of a party's probable response to anticipated situations. It is this feature of threats that introduces the well-known problem of credibility. An actor employing threats as a form of coercion must convince the intended victim that he is willing (or at least that there is some probability that he is willing) to act in such a way as to harm himself (in addition to the victim) in the event that the threat fails (Schelling, 1960). Additionally, any threats used to exert pressure toward Korean unification would have to be compellant threats rather than deterrent threats. That is, they would have to be designed to force an adversary to take positive steps with regard to unification; it would not be sufficient simply to deter an adversary from initiating unwanted actions (Schelling, 1966: 69–78).

Neither the ROK nor the DPRK possesses great threat potential that can be brought to bear on the issue of reunification. Military threats are of course possible, but they are not credible under current circumstances. It would be virtually impossible for one side to convince the other that it would launch a large-scale first strike in the absence of fundamental concessions relating to unification. Beyond this, the repertoire of available threats is narrow. Threats involving subversive interventions in the internal affairs of the ROK or the DPRK are of limited potential simply because each side lacks the capability to initiate truly effective subversive activities in the other's domain. And the fact that the ROK and DPRK engage in such a low level of transactions in other realms drastically limits the ability of each to formulate meaningful threats relating to unification. Parties having little or nothing to do with each other will have a hard time finding ways to punish each other (Young, 1969).

An alternative approach to coercion focuses on the use of sanctions rather than threats. Threats suggest that harm will be inflicted unless the target makes an effort to do what the threatener demands. Sanctions involve the actual imposition of harm on the target coupled with a promise that the sanctions will cease as soon as the target conforms to the demands of the party imposing the sanctions (Schelling, 1966: esp. Ch. 1). The essential idea underlying sanctions is that it may be possible to break an adversary's will by actually inflicting harm on him. While an adversary may give in to avoid being injured in the case of a threat, he is expected to give in to gain relief from ongoing harm in the case of sanctions. Nonetheless, the practical problems associated with the use of sanctions to promote Korean unification are much the same as those restricting the use of threats. Each side is capable of making life difficult for the other with respect to matters like military spending and subversive harassment. Thus, the DPRK spends roughly 15 percent of its GNP to maintain parity with the South in terms of military capabilities, and the ROK has paid a high price in both material and intangible terms to protect itself from subversive incursions launched by the North. But sanctions of this sort have proved totally insufficient to force either side into offering significant concessions relating to the terms of Korean unification. Once again, the fact that the level of transactions is so low between the ROK and the DPRK minimizes the opportunities for either side to bring effective pressure to bear on the other.

The use of strategic moves constitutes another avenue for those wishing to force their adversaries into submitting to specific demands (Young, 1968: Ch. 2).[14] The fundamental idea here is to manipulate the options available to an adversary to one's own advantage. In chess, for example, victory can be obtained by maneuvering the opponent into a situation in which he is forced to choose between sacrificing his queen and protecting his king from impending checkmate. More broadly, strategic moves involve efforts to alter the relationship, thereby changing the options or incentives of one's opponent(s). This may be done in a variety of ways, such as entering into new alliances, finding alternative sources of raw materials or labor, devising ways to get along without certain goods or services, and so forth. How can stratagems of this sort be brought to bear on the case of Korean unification? The obvious possibilities include (1) efforts on the part of the ROK or the DPRK to isolate the other diplomatically and (2) attempts by each side to outperform the other overwhelmingly in economic terms (George, Hall, and Simons, 1971). Success with either of these stratagems would allow the more powerful side to present the other with the options of unification on favorable terms or relegation to pariah status in the international community. In fact, both the ROK and the DPRK have made vigorous efforts to pursue these stratagems. But neither side has been able to gain a decisive advantage either in diplomatic terms or in economic terms, and there is no reason to expect dramatic changes in this situation during the foreseeable future.

A final class of coercive stratagems involves the manipulation of risks. Simply put, a party engaged in strategic interaction can deliberately initiate a dangerous dynamic (for example, a situation whose structure resembles that of the game of chicken) or precipitate a major crisis in the hope of exploiting the resultant tension or confusion to its own advantage (Schelling, 1960: esp. Ch. 7–8). This is obviously a dangerous tack to take at any level of human interaction; crises in interpersonal relations can lead to highly destructive outcomes and crises between states periodically lead to wars. Yet crises are also periods of opportunity during which actors may be jolted out of rigid approaches to problems. What is more, they may be exploited effectively by actors who are risk seekers (as opposed to those who are risk-averse) or who are particularly skillful at dealing with the pressures and confusion of crises (Snyder, 1972). Yet it is hard to see much scope for risk manipulation as a successful coercive stratagem in conjunction with the problem of Korean unification. Once again, the only suitable stage for such tactics would involve relatively large-scale military confrontations. Under current conditions, such confrontations would almost certainly lead to a reaffirmation of the preexisting military stalemate or to escalation involving a shift from nonviolent coercion to violence.

Coercion is employed widely, as a supplement or as an alternative to ordinary bargaining, by those seeking to resolve severe conflicts of interests. In fact, many social institutions rest on some sort of coercive relationship, despite the fact that it is often regarded as tactless or threatening to emphasize this fact. Certainly, coercive activities have been prominent in relations between the ROK and the DPRK, though the two sides have refrained from large-scale violence for a generation. Nonetheless, coercion is not a promising approach to the problem of Korean unification. The scope for the deployment of coercive tactics is severely limited in this case. The two sides have developed more or less effective counters to each other's coercive ploys. And the costs of unsuccessful coercive diplomacy are high. This is obviously true with respect to the direct costs of military preparedness or defense against potential subversive incursions. But it is important to notice the indirect costs of coercion as well. It is hard to avoid the conclusion that the prevalence of coercion in the ROK/DPRK relationship severely hinders efforts to achieve Korean unification through ordinary bargaining or problem solving.

## PROBLEM SOLVING

Both bargaining and coercive diplomacy are, as Anatol Rapoport has put it, strategic approaches to peaceful unification in Korea. They are "dominated by a theory of rational decision extending to situations involving conflict" (Rapoport, 1966a: 88). As such, these approaches to unification direct attention to the efforts of individual parties to maximize their own gains in the face of more or less severe conflicts of interest.

Both bargaining and coercive diplomacy constitute highly influential approaches to interdependent decisionmaking. This is perhaps especially true at the international level where feelings of social solidarity are comparatively weak. But these approaches have also evoked sharp criticism and a persistent search for alternatives. One attractive alternative is often discussed under the rubric of problem solving.[15] The emphasis here is on reconceptualizing relationships among parties to focus on the identification of common problems as well as on the development of cooperative or integrative techniques to be used in the search for solutions to such problems. As before, we assume the existence of separate actors capable of behaving in a purposive fashion. Further, we continue to focus on situations involving interdependent decisionmaking in the sense that outcomes affecting all the parties (for example, divorce, inflation, war) are seen as products of the choices of each of the parties. The focus of problem solving, however, is a search for goals to be achieved through joint efforts together with techniques for coordinating behavior in the interests of avoiding mutual losses.[16] An arms race, for example, can be approached as a common problem requiring effective coordination to realize the mutual benefits associated with arms reductions rather than as a game or competitive situation in which each side focuses primarily on the search for winning tactics or ways to gain the upper hand over the opponent.[17] Similarly, the members of a society may come to regard inflation as a common problem solvable only through genuine restraint and coordination on the part of all rather than as a situation in which each individual group within society endeavors to stay ahead of the spiral of inflation by extracting better terms from other groups. The fundamental perspective of problem solving, therefore, contrasts sharply with the strategic perspective underlying the analysis of bargaining tactics and coercive stratagems.

Needless to say, problem solving as an approach to interdependent decisionmaking can only succeed under somewhat restrictive conditions. Above all, the parties must be able to break out of the strategic mode of thought, which is pervasive in most cultures, in order to redirect their attention to common problems and to explore specific techniques of problem solving. In cultures placing a heavy emphasis on competition and individual success, this will ordinarily require a gestalt shift or a paradigm switch (Burton, 1979: Ch. 8). Such occurrences are uncommon in the absence of some shock or system failure (for example, a marital crisis, an economic depression, a lost war).[18] Even if the parties are able to shift from an emphasis on conflicts of interest to a concern for common problems, they must develop a capacity to engage in a meaningful dialog with each other. Little will be gained if the parties approach problem solving as an exercise in propaganda (continuously articulating rigid proposals that are obviously one-sided) or as a dangerous process in which they open themselves up to subtle forms of exploitation. Rather, problem solving requires an openness to new ideas and a willingness to engage in exploratory discussions in the absence of any predetermined agenda; it cannot produce constructive results among those whose main concern is to induce or compel others to accept some system of propositions or institutional arrangements worked out in advance (Rokeach, 1960).

Under the circumstances, it is hardly surprising that this approach to interdependent decisionmaking has given rise to a growing interest in the development of creative problem-solving techniques and in constructive roles for third parties. Techniques like simulation exercises, role playing, imaging, and the articulation of relevant utopias may help all parties to gain perspective on common problems as well as to break free from inflexible preconceptions, especially those that are embedded beneath the surface of conscious thought.[19] For their part, third parties can serve to referee problem-solving sessions, introduce specific techniques previously unfamiliar to the parties, and take steps to prevent the parties from falling back into a strategic mode of thought (Burton, 1969). In the context of problem solving, the emphasis will ordinarily be on nondirective third party activities. Thus, appropriate models are the therapist in interpersonal situations and the mediator in intergroup situations rather than the arbitrator or the judge presiding over an adversarial proceeding.[20]

Problem solving has gained considerable popularity as an approach to interpersonal difficulties. It has even been used successfully as a means of dealing with group situations (for example, problems of improving office productivity). Yet this does not license the conclusion that problem solving will turn out to be the key to the problem of Korean unification. In general, political settings are not conducive to the successful introduction of problem-solving techniques.[21] Political leaders who experiment with problem solving are likely to become vulnerable to domestic opponents arguing that they are taking unacceptable risks in the realm of security. There is an entrenched tradition of worst-case thinking among those who are influential in the realm of interstate relations. As a result, decisionmakers dealing with security issues will typically experience unusually severe barriers impeding any switch from a strategic mode of thought to a problem-solving perspective (White, 1968: esp. Part 3). Additionally, these decisionmakers will be particularly susceptible to what Irving Janis (1972) has called groupthink, a phenomenon that is antithetical to the exploratory attitude and openness required for successful problem solving.

What is more, there are special impediments to the use of problem solving embedded in the Korean case. Both the ROK and, especially, the DPRK exhibit a marked propensity to act on the basis of ideological formulas. Their interactions therefore have a stilted quality, and there is little scope for unstructured dialog between representatives of the two parties. Moreover, it is hard to avoid the conclusion that the relationship between these parties is deeply affected by residual antagonisms and bitterness emanating from the 1950–53 war (Scalapino, 1976). Much the same can be said about the tendency of these parties to mistrust each other. A generation of hostility between the ROK and the DPRK has left the leaders of these parties with a deep-seated habit of assuming the worst about each other when it comes to seeking agreement on terms for the political unification of the peninsula. Under the circumstances, both sides are more comfortable with the outlook underlying hard bargaining or even coercive diplomacy than they are with the orientation of problem solving toward free-form exercises and creative efforts to restructure thought in the search for solutions to common problems.

It follows that success in the application of problem-solving techniques to the case of Korean unification would require major shifts in the outlooks of both the ROK and DPRK. Of course, it would be a mistake to rule out this prospect. Few observers predicted the recent course of Egyptian-Israeli relations prior to 1978. And internal upheavals in the ROK coupled with a succession crisis in the DPRK could easily bring to power leaders on both sides who would see great attractions in the problem-solving approach as a means of breaking the costly deadlock that has characterized North/South relations for a generation.[22] At the same time, current conditions in the Korean peninsula offer no clearcut basis for hope regarding this prospect. Though it is sometimes hard to predict the exact timing of an impending gestalt shift, there are few indications in the Korean peninsula today that we are even approaching the point at which a shift of this sort becomes a distinct possibility.

## SPONTANEOUS UNIFICATION

Under some conditions, political unification may result from the interactive behavior of two or more parties without any individual party consciously pursuing this goal. As Friedrich Hayek has put it, "there exist orderly structures which are the product of the action of many men but are not the result of human design" (Hayek, 1973: 37). Without doubt, any resultant political order would fall toward the informal/decentralized end of the spectrum described at the outset of this chapter—"such orders . . . do not obtrude themselves on our senses but have to be traced by our intellect" (Hayek, 1973: 38). But it would clearly qualify as a form of political unification nonetheless.

Could some such dynamic lead to peaceful unification in the case of Korea? Two distinct cases are worthy of consideration in this context: (1) coordination by convention and (2) functional integration. As the recent literature on public choice has demonstrated, purposive actors often fail to reap mutual gains or suffer mutual losses because of coordination problems.[23] Well-known paradigms of such problems include prisoner's dilemma, the tragedy of the commons, and the logic of collective action.[24] In all these cases, behavior that appears rational (in the value-maximizing sense) from the point of view of the individual actor leads inexorably to outcomes that are suboptimal (and sometimes disastrous for all parties concerned) (Rapoport, 1960: Part 2; cf. Barry and Hardin, 1982).

Social conventions typically arise in conjunction with efforts on the part of groups of actors to avoid, or at least to ameliorate, these coordination problems (Hardin, 1982: Ch. 10–14). Such conventions are guides to action which individual actors treat as operative without examining their merits on a case-by-case basis. While conventions of this type are seldom articulated explicitly in the form of social contracts, they may become institutionalized in the sense that they are widely recognized as operative and that they serve effectively to coordinate the expectations of groups of actors. Just as the superpowers have reached tacit understandings concerning certain conventions of crisis,[25] the ROK and the DPRK might well arrive at conventional understandings governing their relationship. Over time, this process could lead to the emergence of a security community, if not some more elaborate form of unification. Note, however, that it would be pointless to pursue this type of political order by articulating detailed and explicit proposals for unification. Coordination by convention is a tacit process whose progress may well be aborted by premature efforts to codify the resultant understandings as formal agreements.

A second approach to spontaneous unification, more familiar to students of international relations, is associated with the literature on functionalism and neofunctionalism.[26] The essential idea here is that cooperative activities or joint ventures initiated in certain limited and ostensibly nonpolitical realms may precipitate a self-propelling process leading to an expanding range of cooperative relations and ultimately to political unification as a means of managing the resultant web of interdependencies. Spelled out under the heading of the logic of spillover, this idea has given rise to a substantial body of theory dealing with economic and political integration (Lindberg and Scheingold, 1971).

Though the perspective of functionalism was originally proposed as an approach to world order, there is no reason to conclude that functional integration cannot occur on a smaller scale. Of course, any process of this type requires a willingness on the part of the participants to initiate low-level cooperative ventures in specific areas. But the logic of spillover does not require the articulation of any comprehensive plans for the negotiation of a "constitutional" contract. Political unification would be the product of a continuous process rather than the subject of an explicit bargain. As in the case of coordination by convention, therefore, this approach to unification does not require any elaborate, formal proposals dealing with the institutional structure of a unified state. In fact, proposals of this sort are antithetical to the dynamic of spillover envisioned in the neofunctionalist scheme of things.

Both these processes of spontaneous unification are apt to fail unless they fall on fertile ground. This is where problems with this strategy of unification begin to become apparent in the case of Korea. To illustrate, a necessary (though not sufficient) condition for either coordination by convention or functional integration is a high level of transactional interdependence among the parties involved.[27] But as I have already indicated, the level of transactions between the ROK and the DPRK is remarkably low, except in a few areas (for example, military incidents along the DMZ) that accentuate friction rather than cooperative activities between the two sides. Similarly, the prospects for spontaneous unification will be much brighter in an environment characterized by economic and sociocultural convergence in contrast to progressive divergence in these terms. This is widely regarded as a key determinant of integration in the case of Europe where the process has been analyzed most systematically. Of course, it is true that the Korean people still constitute a single nation, a condition that is certainly favorable from the point of view of spontaneous unification. But the fact that the two systems are drifting apart with regard to their economic and social institutions can only serve to reduce the prospects for spontaneous unification with the passage of time.

What is more, coordination by convention and functional integration are apt to work best under conditions of internal stability and cohesion within the participating parties.[28] The resultant atmosphere of confidence will allow the parties to approach their interactions in a cooperative spirit without fear of being attacked within domestic political arenas. Equally important, internal stability and cohesion will permit leaders on each side to refrain from accentuating external conflicts in order to maintain control internally or to divert attention from domestic problems. Here, too, the Korean case seems far from promising. The DPRK may well experience a succession crisis of considerable magnitude during the near future, and domestic conditions within the ROK are not currently conducive to stability. Moreover, it is apparent that each side has exploited North/South conflict for years as a justification for directive and somewhat authoritarian policies within its own political system. Under the circumstances, both the DPRK and the ROK exhibit a pronounced tendency to act in such a way as to provoke a sense of insecurity in the other, a propensity that is hardly conducive to the achievement of unification through spontaneous processes.

Coordination by convention and functional integration are attractive processes. They are informal. They are gradual; no leap of faith of the sort involved in the articulation of a "constitutional" contract is required. They do not require dramatic policy reversals or initiatives of the sort that would have to precede negotiated unification. Consequently, it would be a mistake to rule out the occurrence of spontaneous unification in the case of Korea. Having said that, however, it must be emphasized that the prospects for spontaneous unification are anything but bright in this case. We now know that coordination problems often prove exceedingly difficult to solve and that the logic of spillover is subject to numerous pitfalls under the best of circumstances. Given both the structural and the political character of the relationship between the ROK and the DPRK, it is evident that any process of spontaneous unification will encounter formidable obstacles in the Korean peninsula.

## THE ROAD AHEAD

The analysis of the preceding sections does not license optimistic conclusions about the prospects for peaceful unification in Korea. On the contrary, any realistic appraisal would have to rate the odds on peaceful unification during the foreseeable future as poor. Yet this analysis does allow us to isolate the critical factors impeding progress toward peaceful unification.

Obviously, the conflict preference structures of the ROK and the DPRK cannot be overlooked. If these preference structures are not (to use the idiom of game theory) strictly opposed, they certainly do indicate that the conflict of interest between the two sides is severe.[29] But what is equally striking is the fact that neither side desires unification enough to take any significant risks in the pursuit of this goal. Perhaps this is merely a reflection of internal doubts or feelings of insecurity within the leadership on both sides. Still, it is hard to imagine any approach to peaceful unification that would protect the parties from all risks while opening up creative opportunities for the development of a new political order in Korea.

The pervasiveness of strategic thinking is another critical factor impeding progress toward Korean unification.[30] Both sides approach the issue in strategic terms, emphasizing the competitive aspect of their relationship and seeking ways to maximize their own gains in the context of bargaining or coercive diplomacy. Each side, naturally enough, fears exploitation at the hands of the other and attributes initiatives on the part of the other to strategic maneuvering rather than to any genuine desire to make progress toward unification. Each party exhibits a continuing propensity to try coercive stratagems, though the scope for nonviolent coercion is severely limited in this case and the costs of unsuccessful ventures in coercive diplomacy are high. Additionally, many ROK and DPRK initiatives couched in terms of North-South relations are actually propaganda moves intended to resolve domestic problems or to win favor with other countries rather than to promote serious dialog regarding peaceful unification. Overall, it is hard to avoid the conclusion that the gestalt of strategic interaction is a key element of the Korean conflict just as it is of the Soviet-American conflict.

Added to these considerations is the fact that the ROK and the DPRK are now diverging quite rapidly in economic and sociocultural terms (Clough, 1978). The two systems have undergone dramatic changes in recent decades. The transformation of the ROK in the period since 1960 is well documented, and it seems likely that changes occurring within the DPRK have been at least as fundamental. At the same time, the lack of contact between the North and the South has created a situation in which changes occurring within the ROK and the DPRK have had almost no impact on each other. In another generation, therefore, it is probable that it will no longer make sense to say that the Korean people form a single nation. At that juncture, the only form of political unification that would be relevant to the Korean case would be the type of pluralistic security community that sometimes arises among friendly nation-states (for example, the Scandinavian countries, the Western European countries, or the United States and Canada).

There are good reasons to doubt whether the leaders of the North or the South are seriously committed to the pursuit of unification on reasonable terms. For purposes of analysis, however, let us suppose that the ROK government is genuinely interested in rethinking its policies and desires to make a concerted effort to achieve peaceful unification at this time. What inferences can we draw from the analysis set forth in this chapter to guide such an effort?

It is critically important to take steps to break out of the paradigm of strategic thinking in dealing with the issue of Korean unification. The ROK leadership should consciously avoid approaching the issue in terms of coercive stratagems, regardless of the propensity of the DPRK to resort to coercive diplomacy from time to time. Similarly, it would help to direct more attention toward productive bargaining in contrast to distributive bargaining or coercive diplomacy. To illustrate, it would be constructive for the ROK to express a genuine interest in the substance, as opposed to the form, of the DPRK's proposal for a Democratic Confederal Republic of Koryo (DCRK).[31] Even more important, the ROK should propose exploratory negotiations with DPRK officials which would not be encumbered by any preset agenda or fixed proposals.[32] It is apparent that the two sides are not currently in a position to bargain seriously over the choice of a specific point on a negotiation set. A more appropriate approach would be a series of informal discussions carried out beyond the glare of publicity and without any pressure to haggle over the terms of explicit but conflicting proposals. One possible outcome of such discussions would be a growing interest on both sides in replacing strategic perspectives with the perspective and techniques of problem solving. Certainly, it would be appropriate for the ROK participants in discussions of this sort to approach Korean unification as a common problem to be resolved through coordination and joint action. Though an effective shift to a problem-solving outlook may prove feasible only in the wake of a severe shock to both sides, it is worth exploring the applicability of the problem-solving alternative even under present conditions.

Equally important is a recognition of the fact that there is no way to make progress toward peaceful unification without taking significant risks of a substantive rather than purely verbal nature. Progress is seldom risk free, and it is fair to say that the essence of leadership in politics is creative risk taking. In this context, the growing strength of the ROK should be regarded as a major asset. After all, the ROK has twice the population of the DPRK, four times the GNP of the DPRK, and a population that shows no signs of vulnerability to subversion on the part of the North (Clough, 1978; Snieder, 1979). If anything, these strengths are increasing rather than declining at the present time. Under the circumstances, the ROK leadership should lead from strength, exhibiting an openness and receptivity toward any proposals that might facilitate progress toward unification. As I suggested in the preceding paragraph, for example, it would do no harm for the ROK to express a genuine interest in the DPRK's proposal for a Confederal Republic of Koryo, despite the propagandistic trappings surrounding the proposal. Ignoring the ideological rhetoric of the proposal, there is much in the basic idea of a DCRK that the ROK could afford to espouse without exposing itself to extreme risks.

In the same vein, I am convinced that the ROK government should initiate a series of unilateral steps designed to demonstrate the seriousness of its interest in peaceful unification. Without doubt, it is hard to design unilateral steps that are meaningful without engendering politically unacceptable risks. Yet, a willingness on the part of one or more parties to proceed unilaterally can play a critical role in breaking logjams arising from incompatible commitments and fears related to face saving or the demonstration of political will.[33] Though it would undoubtedly be desirable to initiate a series of unilateral steps sequentially over a period of time, I would advocate serious consideration of the following steps:[34]

1. *Recognition.* The ROK government could announce formally that it recognizes the DPRK as the legitimate government of North Korea and express its willingness to exchange diplomatic representatives with the DPRK.

2. *Propaganda.* The ROK government could studiously avoid articulating propagandistic proposals relating to unification (this would include many of the 1982 proposals) or taking other propagandistic steps even when such initiatives might seem politically beneficial.

3. *Outside actors.* The ROK government could encourage the United States and Japan to recognize the DPRK formally and to take any reasonable steps to increase diplomatic and economic relations with the DPRK.

4. *Joint ventures.* The ROK government could propose joint ventures to the DPRK (for example, in the area of offshore oil and gas development) in much the same fashion that Japan has approached the Soviet Union and the People's Republic of China.

5. *Arms freeze.* The ROK government could initiate a unilateral freeze on the acquisition, production, and deployment of new military capabilities, an-

nouncing that it would continue the freeze so long as there was no indication of any large-scale expansion of the DPRK's military capabilities.

6. *U.S. troops.* The ROK government could call for a significant reduction of U.S. troops in the peninsula (say, 10,000 to 12,000), signaling the seriousness of its interest in peaceful unification without giving up the deterrent value of the presence of U.S. forces.

## POSTSCRIPT

The conditions governing peaceful unification in the Korean peninsula have not changed in any fundamental way during the last five years. The two Koreas continue to drift apart in socioeconomic and cultural terms, and the level of contact between them remains low. Yet it would be wrong to overlook some hopeful developments pertaining to this issue. The political upheaval in the ROK during 1987–88 surely reflects a profound opposition to authoritarian politics and signifies a growing unwillingness on the part of the public to accept the conflict with the DCRK as a valid excuse for the imposition of political restrictions in the South. The government of Roh Tae Woo may well adopt a pragmatic stance that is compatible with efforts to expand a variety of functional contacts with the North in contrast to grand (and largely propagandistic) schemes for political unification by "constitutional" contract. The DCRK shows increasing interest in cutting down its heavy burden of defense spending as well as in reducing its isolation from much of the rest of the world. The growing friendship between the United States and China coupled with the renewed detente between the Soviet Union and the United States suggests that the great powers are not likely to interfere with indigenous efforts to promote political unification between the ROK and the DCRK. If anything, the great powers can be expected to react benignly to increased contact between the two Koreas.

While none of this offers any assurance of success, it does indicate that the 1988 Olympic Games offer an attractive opportunity for new initiatives aimed at alleviating tension and expanding contact between the ROK and the DCRK. I continue to believe that the ROK must take the lead in developments along these lines. The fact that the Olympic Games will be staged largely in the South merely reinforces the reasons for this belief set forth in the body of this chapter. Concretely, the ROK government might take the following steps to make use of this opportunity creatively. It could adopt a generous and relaxed attitude toward the Olympic Games themselves, allowing the DCRK to play a prominent role in staging Olympic events and permitting visitors from other countries to cross the border between the two Koreas freely. It could seize the occasion of the Olympic Games to announce one or more unilateral initiatives of the sort described in this essay. These might include unusually generous offers for economic cooperation with the North. But the most dramatic step would surely be the announcement of a schedule for the withdrawal of a significant number of U.S. troops stationed in Korea. Additionally, the ROK could propose the establishment of a Korean Forum in which representatives of the two Koreas could meet informally on a continuing basis. Because this Forum should emphasize productive bargaining and problem solving, it would be inappropriate to articulate any elaborate proposal for Korean unification in connection with the establishment of the Forum. Rather, the ROK should indicate a willingness to talk openly and constructively about all issues pertaining to Korea in the Forum without any preconceptions or prior expectations about the outcome. The analysis set forth in this chapter certainly does not license undue optimism about the prospects for success with such a program of initiatives. Given the conditions prevailing in the Korean peninsula today, however, it would be unfortunate not to make the effort.

## NOTES

1. For a range of perspectives on these links consult Deutsch and Foltz (1963) and Pye and Verba (1965).

2. For a similar conception of violence see Schelling (1966). This conception differs from that articulated by many structuralists (for example, Johan Galtung) who use the term "violence" to encompass a variety of situations not involving any physical destruction of life or property.

3. On the concept of a "constitutional" contract, see Buchanan (1975: Ch. 4).

4. For a comprehensive survey see Young (1975).

5. For extended discussions consult Gross (1969) and Schelling (1960).

6. For a particularly clear exposition see Rapoport (1966b: Ch. 8).

7. In my judgment, this criticism is applicable to many of the proposals advanced by both the ROK and the DPRK, including those outlined in President Chun Doo-Hwan's "New Year Policy Statement" of January 22, 1982 (Chun, 1982).

8. See also Walton and McKersie (1965) in which this sort of bargaining is labeled "integrative bargaining."

9. See Schelling (1960: Ch. 2) for concrete examples in which the removal of options actually improves the prospects of reaching agreement.

10. For a discussion of this possibility in the context of arms control negotiations see Schelling and Halperin (1961).

11. For a broader study of neutralization see Black et al. (1968).

12. For a range of perspectives on coercion consult Pennock and Chapman (1972).

13. A highly sophisticated analysis of threats appears in Ellsberg (1975).

14. But note that Schelling (1960: Ch. 5) uses the phrase "strategic moves" more broadly to encompass all classes of coercive stratagems.

15. For an early discussion of the generic idea of problem solving see March and Simon (1958: 177–82). On problem solving as an approach to conflict resolution at the international level see Burton (1979).

16. For a discussion of specific problem-solving tactics see Fisher (1969).

17. For a penetrating analysis of alternative ways to think about arms races see Rapoport (1960).

18. For a well-known discussion of the links between crises and scientific revolutions see Kuhn (1970).

19. On the articulation of relevant utopias see Mendlovitz (1975).

20. On the intrinsic problems of adversary processes as techniques of conflict resolution see Frank (1949: esp. Ch. 1–7).

21. Nonetheless, several well-known students of conflict resolution (for example, John Burton, Herbert Kelman) have taken a special interest in the application of problem-solving techniques to highly politicized situations.

22. The costs in terms of military preparedness alone have been enormous (Snieder, 1979).

23. For a survey of the contemporary public choice literature presented in easily accessible terms see Frohlich and Oppenheimer (1978).

24. All these paradigms are discussed in a sophisticated fashion by Russell Hardin (1982). As Hardin points out, the problems captured in these paradigms all exhibit the same basic structure in logical terms.

25. See Bell (1971) on the crisis behavior of the superpowers.

26. For a sophisticated review see Haas (1964: esp. Part I).

27. On transactional (as well as other forms of) interdependence see Cooper (1968) and Keohane and Nye (1977: Ch. 1–2).

28. On the application of this proposition to the case of Korea see Burton (1975).

29. For a broader discussion of the concept "conflict of interest" see Axelrod (1970).

30. For a rich discussion of the pitfalls of strategic thinking see Rapoport (1964).

31. See Appendix A in this volume.

32. In this context, President Chun Doo-Hwan's proposal of June 5, 1981, for a South-North summit meeting seems constructive. See Appendix B in this volume.

33. For a discussion of the value of unilateral steps in conjunction with the pursuit of arms control measures see Osgood (1962: esp. Ch. 5).

34. The steps outlined here are meant to be illustrative only. It would be desirable to devote additional time and resources to refining these options and identifying other feasible unilateral steps.

## REFERENCES

Axelrod, Robert. (1970). *Conflict of Interest*. Chicago: Markham.
Barry, Brian, and Hardin, Russell, eds. (1982). *Rational Man and Irrational Society?* Beverly Hills, CA: Sage.

Bell, Coral. (1971). *The Conventions of Crisis*. London: Oxford University Press.

Black, Cyril E., et al. (1968). *Neutralization and World Politics*. Princeton, NJ: Princeton University Press.

Buchanan, James M. (1975). *The Limits of Liberty*. Chicago: University of Chicago Press.

Burton, John. (1969). *Conflict and Communication*. London: Macmillan.

———. (1975). "Alternatives to Confrontation: North-South Korean Relations," *Korean Journal of International Studies*, 6 (1): 11–16.

———. (1979). *Deviance, Terrorism, and War*. New York: St. Martin's.

Chun Doo-Hwan. (1982). *New Year Policy Statement*. Seoul: Republic of Korea.

Clough, Ralph N. (1978). "Internal Trends in the Two Koreas," paper presented at the Woodrow Wilson International Center for Scholars, April 6.

Cooper, Richard N. (1968). *The Economics of Interdependence*. New York: McGraw-Hill.

Deutsch, Karl W., and Foltz, William J., eds. (1963). *Nation Building*. New York: Atherton.

Deutsch, Karl W., et al. (1957). *Political Community and the North Atlantic Area*. Princeton, NJ: Princeton University Press.

Ellsburg, Daniel. (1975). "The Theory and Practice of Nuclear Blackmail." In Oran R. Young, ed., *Bargaining*, pp. 343–63. Urbana, IL: University of Illinois Press.

Fisher, Roger. (1969). *International Conflict for Beginners*. New York: Harper & Row.

Frank, Jerome. (1949). *Courts on Trial*. Princeton, NJ: Princeton University Press.

Frohlich, Norman, and Oppenheimer, Joe A. (1978). *Modern Political Economy*. Englewood Cliffs, NJ: Prentice-Hall.

George, Alexander L., Hall, David K., and Simons, William R. (1971). *The Limits of Coercive Diplomacy*. Boston: Little, Brown.

Gross, John. (1969). *The Economics of Bargaining*. New York: Basic Books.

Haas, Ernst B. (1964). *Beyond the Nation State*. Stanford, CA: Stanford University Press.

Hardin, Russell. (1982). *Collective Action*. Baltimore: Johns Hopkins Press.

Hayek, Friedrich A. (1973). *Rules and Order*. Chicago: University of Chicago Press.

Janis, Irving L. (1972). *Victims of Groupthink*. Boston: Houghton Mifflin.

Keohane, Robert O., and Nye, Joseph S. (1977). *Power and Interdependence*. Boston: Little, Brown.

Kuhn, Thomas S. (1970). *The Structure of Scientific Revolutions*, 2nd ed. Chicago: University of Chicago Press.

Levy, Marion J., Jr. (1972). *Modernization: Latecomers and Survivors*. New York: Basic Books.

Lindberg, Leon N., and Scheingold, Stuart A., eds. (1971). *Regional Integration: Theory and Research*. Cambridge, MA: Harvard University Press.

Luce, R. Duncan, and Raiffa, Howard. (1957). *Games and Decisions*. New York: Wiley.

March, James G., and Simon, Herbert A. (1958). *Organizations*. New York: Wiley.

Mendlovitz, Saul H., ed. (1975). *On the Creation of a Just Order.* New York: Free Press.

Osgood, Charles E. (1962). *An Alternative to War or Surrender.* Urbana, IL: University of Illinois Press.

Pennock, J. Roland, and Chapman, John W., eds. (1972). *Coercion.* New York: Atherton. (Vol. 14 of *Nomos.*)

Pye, Lucien W., and Verba, Sidney, eds. (1965). *Political Culture and Political Development.* Princeton, NJ: Princeton University Press.

Rapoport, Anatol. (1960). *Fights, Games, and Debates.* Ann Arbor: University of Michigan Press.

———. (1964). *Strategy and Conscience.* New York: Schocken.

———. (1966a). "Strategic and Non-Strategic Approaches to Problems of Security and Peace." In Kathleen Archibald, ed., *Strategic Interaction and Conflict.* Berkeley: University of California Press.

———. (1966b). *Two-Person Game Theory.* Ann Arbor: University of Michigan Press.

Rokeach, Milton. (1960). *The Open and the Cold Mind.* New York: Basic Books.

Scalapino, Robert A. (1976). "The Two Koreas—Dialogue or Conflict?" In William J. Barnds, ed. *The Two Koreas in East Asian Affairs*, pp. 60–112. New York: New York University Press.

Schelling, Thomas C. (1960). *The Strategy of Conflict.* Cambridge, MA: Harvard University Press.

———. (1966). *Arms and Influence.* New Haven, CT: Yale University Press.

Schelling, Thomas C., and Halperin, Morton. (1961). *Strategy and Arms Control.* New York: Twentieth Century Fund.

Snieder, Richard L. (1979). "Prospects for Korean Security." In *Asian Security in the 1980's*, pp. 7–20. Washington, DC: Office of the Assistant Secretary of Defense for International Security Affairs.

Snyder, Glenn H. (1972). "Crisis Bargaining." In Charles F. Hermann, ed., *International Crises*, pp. 217–56. New York: Free Press.

Walton, Richard E., and McKersie, Robert B. (1965). *A Behavioral Theory of Labor Negotiations.* New York: McGraw-Hill.

White, Nathan. (1978). "The Necessity for a German Solution to the Korean Problem," *Korea and World Affairs*, 2 (Fall): 349–68.

White, Ralph K. (1968). *Nobody Wanted War.* Garden City, NY: Doubleday.

Young, Oran R. (1968). *The Politics of Force.* Princeton, NJ: Princeton University Press.

———. (1969). "Interdependencies and World Politics," *International Journal*, 24 (Autumn): 727–50.

Young, Oran R., ed. (1975). *Bargaining: Formal Theories of Negotiation.* Urbana, IL: University of Illinois Press.

# 7 The Political Feasibility Approach to Korean Reunification
### Dae-Sook Suh

Voluminous works have been published on Korean unification, and numerous conferences have been held to discuss the problems related to Korean unification. Many scholars and government officials from both North and South Korea have devised methods and proposed policies to reunite the divided country. However, the country still remains divided after four decades of discussion and policy implementation.[1]

In fact, because of what has transpired—the Korean War in the 1950s, the complete severance of any contact during the 1960s, and the limited dialogue in the 1970s that strengthened the respective regimes by consolidating their positions—the prospect for reunification in the 1980s seems more remote than in the latter half of the 1940s, when the country was first divided. It is true that the international political environment that divided the country has changed substantially, considering the Sino-Soviet conflict, the normalization of Japanese-Korean relations, and the Sino-American rapprochement, to mention only a few changes, but the domestic environment in both North and South Korea for reuniting the divided sectors seems to have worsened.

Under the leadership of Kim Il Sung, North Korea has put forth a hardline policy designed to "liberate" the southern half of the country. The goal of this policy was to weaken the South Korean political system so that the North could reunify the country under its banner of Communism. Since the unsuccessful conclusion of the Korean War, the North has tried to assassinate South Korean political leaders, incite political unrest by supporting dissident groups and students, and has dug tunnels across the demilitarized zone to apply relentless pressures.[2] However, such hardline policy has not achieved its goal.

Throughout the five post-World War II republics in the South, the leaders of the South have taken strong anti-Communist stances, trying to keep the more aggressive North Koreans at bay by strengthening their military forces. In doing so, they have asked for and benefitted from the U.S. military presence in South Korea, and advocated a gradual and step-by-step approach to the problem of national unification. The South Korean reunification policy in essence was a policy of peaceful reunification, but it was impractical and impossible to implement.[3]

Regardless of the merits of these policies, what is most apparent is that both North and South Korean unification policies have not achieved their intended goal, because the country still remains divided. More than ample time has passed for each side to reevaluate their policy for Korean unification. This is not an effort to analyze the failure of the past unification policies of North and South Korea. Nor is this an effort to advocate a new policy for each side to implement. Rather, the purpose of this chapter is to propose a number of hypotheses for change that would be conducive for the unification of Korea. This is a discussion of the type of changes that must be brought about in both the North and South Korean domestic environment in order to make them conducive to unification.

In this chapter, I would like to propose five such changes as being conducive to unification. The first is the institution of genuinely democratic processes of government in both North and South Korea. The second is a more balanced or equal economic development than the current imbalance between North and South Korean economic development. The third is the growth of a more pluralistic political system, particularly in ideological orientation, that would not cling to single ideologies, such as *chuch'e* or anti-Communism. The fourth is the balanced reduction of military forces. The fifth is the effort to create a social environment that would seek a unifying commonality in each society's tradition and culture rather than emphasize the past that divides them.

To be sure, these are difficult propositions, but except for an outright military conquest of one by the other that would subjugate one sector to the other, these difficult processes must take place before a durable unification can be realized. For all that needs to be done for Korean reunification, these propositions are but first steps to be taken by each side to achieve unification.

## DEMOCRATIZING KOREA

After experiencing the rise and fall of five different republics, South Korea in the latter half of the 1980s seems to have instituted a democratic process of government in the sixth republic. All South Korean political leaders from the first to the fifth republics were authoritarian leaders, and they were busy maintaining their own style of authoritarian government. The first republic was toppled by a student demonstration that demanded change from the authoritarian rule of Syngman Rhee to a more efficient economic development under a democratic rule, and the second republic was crushed by a military coup for its incompetence and in the name of the national reconstruction of Korea. Young military leaders did bring about economic development during the third and the fourth republics under Park Chung Hee, but his rule can hardly be called a democratic one. Still another military coup created the fifth republic after the assassination of Park, but authoritarian rule continued.[4]

During all these republics, every leader of Korea advocated "Korean reunification" as the foremost objective of their rule, but none has seriously considered devising policies to implement this national goal. Knowing full well the difficulties in bringing North Koreans to conduct dialogue, the leaders of South Korea paid lip service to the question of national reunification, and went about the task of building the southern half of the country. However, the political system they have built in the South is more an authoritarian than a democratic system of government.

While Kim Il Sung has ruled the northern half of the country for the past four decades, the political system that he has built in the North resembles more his personal kingdom than a socialist or communist system of government where the dictatorship of the proletariat would prevail. Except for the time of the Korean War, when he attempted to reunify the country militarily, Kim's policy for national reunification was a hard-line policy of subjugating the people of the southern half of Korea under his rule by any means short of military action. For this policy, Kim advocated close international ties along with a revolution in the South, but most importantly he advocated building a firm revolutionary base in the northern half of the country.[5]

However, the firm revolutionary base he built in the northern half of the country is not a democratic system of government, not even a haven for the workers and peasants, and certainly not a *Democratic People's* Republic as advertised in the name of his country. Rather, it resembles more a totalitarian regime where he rules with absolute authority, and where the people are there to serve the supreme leader and his son, who is about to succeed him. No individuals or interest groups in the North, for example, articulate or aggregate their interests through the political system.

Kim, too, claimed that the foremost objective of his republic is to peacefully reunify the country, but those who heard that call for more than three decades since the Korean War, no longer hold him respon- sible for his claim. What is more readily identifiable in North Korean politics is his establishment and maintenance of a totalitarian system of government, rather than his vow of peaceful national reunification.

It is contended here that both the authoritarian regimes of the South and the totalitarian regime of the North are detrimental to achieving reunification of the country. I believe that an institution of democratic processes of government in both North and South Korea would be more conducive to national reunification.

Compared with authoritarian or totalitarian regimes, a democratic system of government would more readily serve the interest of the people, and the people of both Koreas do long for their national re- unification. At times, it seems that authoritarian or totalitarian leaders tend to preserve their own political control, thus solidifying the divi- sion, at the expense of the needs and demand of the people. Also, when and if both North and South Korea were to institute a truly democratic system of government, the likelihood of the two systems converging is far greater than the current trend of continued development into di- vergent political systems. Democratic systems of government would be able to find common grounds upon which the two sides could agree, as well as the grounds upon which each is willing to yield, so long as the principle of democratic governance is maintained.

This argument, of course, assumes that the institution of democratic processes of government must occur on both sides, though not neces- sarily simultaneously. When and if the sixth republic institutes the democratic process of governing in the South, the South would be more prepared for reunification than the North, and if the South can refine its democratic system, this may indeed give incentives to the gener- ation that will succeed the rule of Kim Il Sung and Kim Jong Il to want to institute a democratic system of government in the North. When it has systematized and functionalized the democratic process, the South can claim with authority that it is the North with its total- itarian rule that hinders the ultimate reunification of Korea. At least this would be more convincing than the current South Korean con- demnation of North Korean reunification policy. South Korea is now on the verge of instituting democratic processes of government in the sixth republic, but the change must also come in North Korea.

## BALANCING THE ECONOMIC DEVELOPMENT

If there is one solid accomplishment that the South Korean author- itarian leaders can point to with pride, it is their rapid economic de- velopment, which began in the 1960s. With the normalization of diplomatic relations with Japan and their participation in the Vietnam conflict, President Park brought a phenomenal economic growth during the 1970s that was unprecedented in Korean history. Compared with the South Korean development, North Korea's multi-year national economic plans, such as the first, second, and the current third seven-year plan, failed to bring the anticipated economic growth that could allow them to compete with their brethren in the South.

Amid effusive praise for their own accomplishments, North Koreans proclaimed with pride that there is nothing in the world for them to envy, and that they are well fed, adequately housed, and wrapped in warm clothes in the winter. However, the fact remains that they default on loans in international markets,[6] and they lag far behind the economic progress made in the South.

Even a conservative comparison of gross national products (GNP) puts the South several times ahead of the North, $800 million for the South to $150 million for the North in mid–1980s; and the per capita GNP of the South is more than double that of the North at $2,000 to $800.[7] In international trade, the comparison becomes more pronounced. Suffice it here to state that there is a significant amount of imbalance in economic development between North and South Korea.

It is my contention that developed and advanced economic systems are more prepared to negotiate and more capable to compromise than economically underdeveloped or backward systems. Economically more advanced systems can readily differentiate their economic structure to meet increased demands and take up new challenges to the system, but economically less developed systems concentrate more on their own development than on cooperating with other systems. At times, underdeveloped economic systems may not have the structure to adjust to new challenges and cannot afford to finance new developments. Thus they become more conservative and hesitant to change. More affluent and economically advanced systems can afford to study and launch new ventures for even larger and more rewarding works, including the feasibility of combined economic ventures between North and South Korea.

It is argued here that the unification of Korea is less likely to occur as long as the pace of economic development is as unbalanced as it is today. The unification of Korea is more likely to occur between two advanced economic systems, when the economic imbalance between North and South Korea is minimized. In other words, the cooperation between two economically advanced systems is more conducive to reunifying the country than between two underdeveloped economic systems, or between one advanced and one underdeveloped economic system. The economic imbalance currently prevailing between North and South Korea is not conducive to Korean reunification. It would be better for reunification if North Korean economic development could match that of South Korea, and both North and South Korea could join the ranks of the world's industrialized and economically advanced nations.

The economic imbalance creates more problems in North-South dialogue than it solves. In fact, past economic cooperation negotiations have failed to bring about their desired results in part because of the significant gap in North-South economic development. The South Korean government, for example, would deal with the North Korean government differently if the North Korean economic development either matched or surpassed that of South Korea. It would be most conducive to Korean reunification if both North and South Korea achieved the status of an advanced industrialized nation, with substantial economic development. For this reason a change in economic development must occur in North Korea.

## PLURALISTIC IDEOLOGICAL ORIENTATION

During the Japanese occupation of Korea, Korean revolutionaries, both Communist and Nationalist, cooperated in the struggle to attain Korean independence. Their anti-Japanese sentiment united Koreans of various ideological persuasions. In fact, when the Korean Provisional Government was first established, its president was an American-educated nationalist, Syngman Rhee, while his Prime Minister, Yi Tong-Hwi, was the head of the Korean Communist Party. There are numerous records in the annals of the Korean revolutionary movement where a Korean nationalist lawyer defended Korean Communists in a court presided over by Japanese judges.[8] Even the Korean anarchists have contributed to the Korean independence movement, joining in anti-Japanese activities.

The current sharp ideological split between North and South Korea developed from the division of Korea after the Second World War. Even after the division, serious efforts were made by ideologically diverse groups to unite the revolutionaries of the left and the right to form a united front for the sake of Korean independence.[9] The seemingly irreconcilable relationships of today emanated from the killings and atrocities committed by both sides during the fratricidal war from 1950 to 1953. It is the unsuccessful conclusion of the war that intensified the hostility between the two sides.

Gradually but surely the North consolidated its political system under the guidance of Marxism and Leninism, under Soviet tutelage, and as Kim Il Sung solidified his power, the Communist institution that he was supposed to build and refine has become a totalitarian regime, ultimately developing into a regime guided by his own ideology called *chuch'e*, a principle of self-reliance. It is this principle, at times referred to as Kimilsungism, that Kim Il Sung and his son Kim Jong Il use to indoctrinate the people of North Korea today.

South Koreans, on the other hand, developed a strong anti-Communist sentiment after the war. The memories of war and the atrocities committed by the Communists during the war contributed much to the South Korean anti-Communist stance. The most stringent anti-Communist laws were passed in part to prevent Communist infiltration from the North to the South. Justifiably, some argue that the South has mounted its heated anti-Communist campaign for self-preservation, to defend itself against the relentless infiltration by North Korean terrorists and agitators from the South, but at the same time the South has also used this law to curb anti-government demonstrations and suppress dissidents who were not Communists.

Such campaigns reached an extreme when scholars and students were prohibited from reading even theoretical works on Marxism and Leninism and the people were forbidden to learn about things North Korean even if they were unrelated to the tenets of Communism. North Korea, on the other hand, has not only indoctrinated its people in the *chuch'e* idea but also prohibited its scholars and students from learning about any other ideas. Today this has degenerated into the preaching of monolithic ideas with religious fervor, and nothing short of absolute subscription and obedience to this idea of *chuch'e* is being allowed in the North.

It is proposed here that this sort of monistic ideology in both North and South Korea is not conducive to Korean unification. Subscription to a single idea may serve the cause of preservation and maintenance for each individual system, but it does not serve the cause of reuniting the two sides. Their monistic ideological orientation is self-serving and self-righteous, and does not serve the cause of reuniting Korea.

Pluralistic ideological orientations must prevail in each domestic political environment before reunification can seriously be discussed. In other words, North Korea should let "the hundred flowers bloom," so to speak, and let the hundred schools of thought contend for the development of Korea. Young people must be allowed to study and learn about non-Communist ideas and scholars must study the utility of other ideas for Korean development.

Similarly, South Korea should ease its strong anti-Communist stance and allow its young people to study and learn about the varieties of Communism, socialism, and other revolutionary ideas—not to encourage them to incite revolution but to better understand their Northern brethren for the cause of reunification. It is true that South Korean anti-Communist laws have been repealed, but ideological control of the South Korean populace is still very strong. Such control should be eased not only to enrich the intellectual content of South Korean society and its political culture, but more importantly to create a domestic environment that is conducive to Korean reunification.

A pluralistic ideological orientation is important to the domestic environment, and it should be created in both North and South Korea. The sixth republic in South Korea may be able to create such an environment without neglecting its security and public safety. Indeed, such an environment may enhance the new republic's image. When Kim Jong Il succeeds his father, he too should consider creating an environment of pluralistic ideological orientation that would be conducive to the reunification of Korea.

## REDUCING THE MILITARY

Since the Korean War, North and South Korea have gradually increased their military forces, ostensibly to defend themselves from each other. Today, North Korea ranks nineteenth and South Korea ranks twenty-third in the leading military powers of the world, and if the two sides are combined, Korea as a nation will be one of the most heavily militarized countries in the world.[10] In an effort to balance military power against each other, North and South Korea have built up their military forces to a degree unprecedented in Korean history.

By the mid–1980s, North Korea had 784,000 people in arms, or nearly 40 out of every 1,000 North Koreans, which ranks them third in the world behind Iraq and Israel. South Korea, with twice the population of the North, has 602,000 people in its armed forces, or approximately 14 out of every 1,000 South Koreans, which ranks them twenty-fifth in the world. In addition, South Korea has maintained at least 40,000 U.S. military personnel in Korea since the Korean War.[11]

North Korea ranks fourth in military expenditures, spending 22.6 percent of its GNP, while South Korea ranks forty-second, spending 5.4 percent of its GNP, but the absolute amount each side spends for military expenditure is quite similar. The North spends $5.2 billion while the South spends $4.6 billion, and if they are combined, Korea would match the military expenditures of the ten most industrialized and economically advanced nations of the world.

Today, both North and South Korea continue to build up their military forces far above and beyond what is needed for Koreans to defend themselves against Koreans, and both sides import in excess of $300 million ($380 million for South Korea in 1985) worth of arms from abroad to improve their current forces. North Koreans are also engaged in arms export to other Third World countries, to the tune of $200 million in 1985, and this constitutes 15 percent of their total exports.

This kind of military buildup for some four decades in Korea has not helped the cause of Korean reunification. Military buildup can contribute to Korean unification only if it creates a complete imbalance in the strength of the armed forces of North and South Korea, in other words, only if the military strength of one side is so powerful that it can achieve reunification either by force or by the threat of force. When the relative balance of military strength is maintained, military buildup has little or no relevance to the reunification of Korea.

Since both sides would maintain a relative balance in military strength, military buildup is not conducive to Korean reunification. All South Korean presidents except Syngman Rhee have advocated the policy of peaceful reunification of Korea, while building up their own armed forces to the extent that they would be able to conquer the North militarily. Similarly, Kim Il Sung has also advocated peaceful reunification of Korea, after he was unsuccessful in his effort to reunify the country militarily in 1950. However, contrary to their pronouncements, both sides have been engaged in a military buildup.

Recently North Korea has announced a unilateral reduction of military forces.[12] Whether such action can be trusted or not is a political question, because such reduction presumes the withdrawal of the United States troops from South Korea. Perhaps the purpose of such an announcement of unilateral reduction is to effect the U.S. troop withdrawal. Furthermore, unilateral reduction is not conducive to unification, except to encourage one regime to subjugate the other. Rather it is more realistic for Korean reunification to reduce simultaneously the level of military forces in both North and South Korea.

A lower level of military strength, rather than high-level military buildup, is more conducive to the reunification of Korea, not simply because such a high level of military buildup has not contributed to the cause of reunification, but because a lower level of military strength would prevent political or military leaders from once again seeking a military solution to the problem of reunification. At least nonmilitary solutions would be more truthful to what they have been advocating for the past three decades, peaceful unification.

Both North and South Korea should enter into a gradual, balanced reduction program that can be checked and verified. Such a reduction program may create an atmosphere of trust and cordiality that would contribute to an environment leading to a serious discussion of reunification. Verification of actual reduction of armed forces would become a good example of what is commonly referred to as a confidence-building measure. When and if such trust and confidence can be established, the U.S. troops should be withdrawn from South Korea. It is easier to imagine the U.S. troop withdrawal resulting from this kind of process rather than from any unilateral reduction of armed forces by North Koreans. The presence of U.S. troops in South Korea is not conducive to the reunification of Korea. The United States may prevent

North Korea from launching another attack on South Korea, but the presence of foreign troops of any kind, be they from the United States, China, or the USSR, does not contribute to the reunification of Korea.

This time around, Korea should be unified by Koreans, without interference or assistance from non-Korean elements. Only then may Korea achieve complete, true independence in a sovereign, unified Korea.

## SEEKING COMMONALITY

Koreans claim one of the longest historical traditions, dating their origin back five millennia. Against this history, the Korean division is indeed a short span of less than a half century, but the hatred, animosity, and hostility developed during the division is intense to say the least. North Korea is known as one of the most isolated and secluded societies in the world. It bars its people from knowing about other peoples and their achievements, thus depriving them of the fruits of human accomplishments. North Koreans know even less about the people and their accomplishments in the South. In fact, North Koreans not only downgrade South Korean achievements, they also fabricate facts to belittle South Koreans.[13]

During the past four decades North Korea reported hardly anything constructive about South Korea. They have not only sent commandos to attempt the assassination of South Korean presidents both within and outside of the Korean peninsula, they have also killed the wife of President Park, and dug tunnels for the purpose of infiltration into South Korea. Of all those North Korean representatives who have visited Seoul for political, economic, and even humanitarian purposes, few have praised South Korean achievements.

Even South Korean plans to host the 1988 summer Olympic Games in Seoul became a target for an anti-South Korean propaganda campaign. North Koreans at first urged their allies to boycott the games, because Seoul was not a fit place for an international sports games to be held, and when they realized that this policy was not feasible, the North appealed to the International Olympic Committee to co-host the summer games, asking for a larger number of games than what the IOC and South Korea were willing to give. This is not simply a bankrupt foreign policy but an un-Korean policy.

South Korea, too, for a long time has denigrated North Korean achievements, barring its people from knowing about developments in North Korea. They taught their children not to trust North Koreans, ridiculing the North Korean leader Kim Il Sung and identifying the North Koreans with evil deeds. The people in South Korea are in general ignorant of what transpires in North Korea. Stringent anti-

Communist laws have restricted South Korean scholars from learning about the North, forbidding the reading or possession of any North Korean publications.

South Koreans for the past four decades have been told by their government that the danger of North Korean military aggression was imminent. To make laudatory remarks about North Korean accomplishments was considered a crime. This sort of fanaticism reached an extreme when the South Koreans collected funds to build what is known as a "peace dam," ostensibly to prevent flooding caused by the destruction of an as yet unconstructed North Korean hydroelectric dam near the border.[14]

These are all manifestations of fanaticism coming from the long separation of an homogeneous people. It is argued here that it is more conducive for Korean reunification for North and South Korea to seek commonality than to denounce and belittle each other's accomplishments. Both groups should seek out and praise those achievements that would benefit both sides, rather than seek out and blame divergent elements that would further consolidate the division.

Intellectually, the two sides should study and learn from each other, to foster the Korean tradition. Politically, each should be magnanimous enough to allow for eccentricities that come primarily from ideological orientation, and seek common strains in their behaviors. In the economic sphere also, instead of comparing each other's accomplishments in order to belittle one another's backwardness, each should seek out the benefit that could be gained for and from each other by developing economic relations. For example, the North should make its natural resources available to the South, and the South should help the North by selling advanced technology that North Koreans cannot acquire but need for development.

Culturally, it would be wise to seek out those aspects of Korean culture that each side has retained and those aspects that each has abandoned in order to foster their own style of new cultural traits. In this connection, it would be important to find new Korean words that each side has developed and uses that are not used by the other side. Similarly, social customs that come from new ideological orientations should be identified and studied, and when applicable should be adopted. In all these societal environments, both sides should seek commonality that would bring the two together, rather than emphasize those differences that would separate them.

In the case of hosting the 1988 Summer Olympic Games by the city of Seoul, the key issue was not the North Korean effort to dissuade its fraternal socialist countries from participating in the Seoul games, because such activity is outright un-Korean. Nor was it the co-hosting of the games in Pyongyang and Seoul, trying to take as many games as possible away from the host city of Seoul to Pyongyang. The Summer Olympic Games was perhaps the biggest international sporting event in Korean history, and North and South Korea should have formed a united Korean team representing both North and South Korea. This is the way to seek commonality.

Seeking commonality would be conducive to reunification. It is safe to assume that a half-century of separation has not done much damage to the substance of Korean culture and societal customs. Rather, the strong animosity expressed in everyday rhetoric is the emotional outburst of political opinion, rather than a deep-rooted cultural expression.

## CONCLUSION

There are other propositions that also would be conducive to Korean national reunification, but the five mentioned above are the most basic and fundamental ones to be considered. If for no other reason than the fact that past policies, however justified from their own standpoint, did not bring the two Koreas together, they should be reevaluated. In fact, the past unification policies have helped each side to further consolidate their own positions vis-à-vis each other. It is about time to redirect the inquiries for Korean national reunification. I would maintain that democratic regimes, advanced and developed economic systems, under pluralistic ideological orientations, a reduced level of military forces, low enough not to be able to subjugate each other militarily, and sincere efforts to seek commonality between the two sides would be more conducive to reunification of Korea.

## NOTES

1. For a bibliographic survey of English-language publications related to the problems of Korean reunification, see Republic of Korea (1986a).

2. For North Korean unification policy, see Kim Il Sung (1969).

3. Discussions of South Korean reunification policy are abundantly available. See, for example, Research Center for Peace and Unification (1978).

4. There are monographs about each republic and its leaders, but few objective analyses of the authoritarian nature of Korean politics. For the present status and direction of the study of Korean politics, see Kim Hak-Chun (1983), a bibliographical study.

5. For a representative speech on this policy, see Kim Il Sung (1976: IV, 77–96).

6. For the latest North Korean default of payments, see *The Wall Street Journal*, July 30, 1987.

7. There are a number of studies done in both the United States and the Republic of Korea. See Republic of Korea (1986b).

8. There are many examples of this kind. Kim Pyong-No, who later became

the first Chief Justice of the Republic of Korea in the South, served as a defense lawyer for Korean Communists at their trial in the late 1920s (Chosen Sotok-ufu, 1930: 34–67).

9. For the records of the post-liberation Korea, see Kim and Kim (1945).

10. For the latest military balance between North and South Korea, see U.S. State Department (1987: 16–19).

11. For the strategic balance in East Asia and the Pacific, see Holshek (1982).

12. See the North Korean announcement of July 22, 1987, in *Pyongyang Times*, August 1, 1987.

13. It is not difficult to find in North Korean magazines and newspapers how poor and downtrodden the South Koreans are, compared with North Korea. Under the title of "Miserable Aspects of South Korea," North Koreans reported on unpaid wages, swindling, trade deficits, and police suppressions. See the details in *Korea Today*, March 1987, p. 43.

14. For the North Korean explanation of the Kungangsan Power Station, see *Pyongyang Times*, January 3, 1987.

## REFERENCES

Chosen Sotokufu. (1930). *Chosen kyosan shugi undo jiken hanketsu hokokusho* [Reports on Incident of the Korean Communist Movement]. Seoul: Chosen Sotokufu.

Holshek, C. J. (1982). *The Military and Strategic Balance: East Asia and the Pacific*. Washington, DC: Woodrow Wilson Center.

Kim Chong-Bom and Kim Tong-Un. (1945). *Haebang chonhu ui Choson chinsang* [Korea Before and After the Liberation]. Seoul: Choson chon'gyong yon'guhoe.

Kim Hak-Chun. (1983). *Hanguk chongch'iron: Yon'gu ui hyonhwanggwa panghyang* [Korean Politics: The Present, Status and Direction of Research]. Seoul: Han'gilsa.

Kim Il Sung. (1969). *Namchoson hyongmyong kaw choguk t'ongil e taehayo* [On South Korean Revolution and National Reunification]. Pyongyang: Choson nodongdang ch'ulp'ansa.

———. (1976). *Chojak sonjip* [Selected Works]. Pyongyang: Choson nondongdang ch'ulp'ansa.

Korea, Republic of. (1986a). *A Bibliographic Catalogue of English Publications*. Seoul: National Unification Board.

———. (1986b). *A Comparative Study of the South and North Korean Economies*. Seoul: National Unification Board.

Research Center for Peace and Unification. (1978). *Korea's Quest for Peaceful Unification: Its History and Prospects for the Future*. Seoul: Research Center for Peace and Unification.

United States, Department of State, Arms Control and Disarmament Agency. (1987). *World Military Expenditures and Arms Transfers, 1986*. Washington, DC: Government Printing Office.

# Appendix A Ten-Point Proposal for a Democratic Republic of Koryo

*Kim Il Sung (1980)*

Our Party considers that the most realistic and reasonable way to reunify the country independently, peacefully and on the principle of great national unity is to bring the north and south together into a confederal state, leaving the ideas and social systems existing in north and south as they are.... (p. 45)

It would be a good idea to call the confederal state the Democratic Confederal Republic of Koryo after a unified state that once existed in our country and is well known to the world, and by reflecting the common aspirations of north and south for democracy.

The DCRK should be a neutral country which does not participate in any political-military alliance or bloc.... (p. 46)

Our Party deems it appropriate that the DCRK should put forward and carry out the following policy:

First, the DCRK should adhere to independence in all state activities and follow an independent policy....(p. 46)

Second, the DCRK should effect democracy throughout the country and in all spheres of society and promote great national unity.... (p. 46)

Third, the DCRK should bring about economic cooperation and exchange between north and south and ensure the development of an independent national economy.... (p. 47)

Fourth, the DCRK should realize north-south exchange and cooperation in the spheres of science, culture and education and ensure uniform progress in the country's science and technology, national culture and arts, and national education.... (p. 47)

Fifth, the DCRK should reopen the suspended transport and communications between north and south and ensure free utilization of the means of transport and communications in all parts of the country.... (p. 48)

Sixth, the DCRK should ensure a stable livelihood for the entire people including the workers, peasants and other working masses and promote their welfare systematically.... (p. 48)

Seventh, the DCRK should remove military confrontation between north and south and form a combined national army to defend the nation from invasion from outside.... The confederal state should reduce the military strength to 100,000 to 150,000 respectively in order to end the military confrontation between north and south and bring fratricidal strife to an end for good. At the same time it is essential to abolish the Military Demarcation Line between north and south, dismantle all military installations in its vicinity, dissolve militia organizations in both parts and prohibit military training of civilians.... (pp. 48–49).

Eighth, the DCRK should defend and protect the rights and interests of all Koreans overseas.... (p. 49)

Ninth, the DCRK should handle properly the foreign relations established by the north and south prior to reunification, and should coordinate the foreign activities of the two regional governments in a unified way.... (p. 49)

Tenth, the DCRK should, as a unified state representing the whole nation, develop friendly relations with all countries of the world and pursue a peaceful foreign policy.... (p. 49)

## REFERENCE

Kim Il Sung. (1980). "Report to the Sixth Congress of the Workers' Party of Korea on the Work of the Central Committee," *Korea Today*, 11, 290: 14–68.

# Appendix B

# Proposal of 20 Pilot Projects to Facilitate National Reconciliation and Democratic Reunification

## Republic of Korea (1982)

( 1) The connecting and opening of a highway between Seoul and Pyongyang as a means of guaranteeing free passage between the South and the North.

( 2) The realization of postal exchanges and reunion of separated families, thereby easing their sufferings.

( 3) The designating and opening of the area north of Mt. Sorak and south of the Diamond Mountain as a joint tourist zone.

( 4) The joint management of homeland visits by overseas Korean residents and their free travel between the two sides by way of Panmunjom.

( 5) The opening of the harbors of Inchon and Chinnampo to facilitate free trade between the South and the North.

( 6) The allowing of free listening to each other's regular radio programs through the removal of tricky propaganda and jamming facilities for the promotion of mutual understanding between the South and the North.

( 7) The participation of North Korean delegations in the 1986 Asian games and 1988 Olympiad, and their entry into the South by way of Panmunjom.

( 8) The allowing of all foreigners wishing to visit the South and the North free access to the two areas by way of Panmunjom.

( 9) The creating of joint fishery zones for the convenience of fishermen of both the South and the North.

(10) The conducting of mutual goodwill visits from various circles, such as politicians, businessmen, youths and students, workers, writers and artists, and sportsmen, to improve relations and foster trust between the South and the North.

(11) The guaranteeing of free press coverage by the journalists of the two sides in each other's area to facilitate the correct reporting of the realities of the societies of the South and the North.

(12) The undertaking of joint research on national history for the purpose of preserving and developing the national culture.

(13) The exchange of goodwill matches in various fields of sports and participation in international games under single delegation between the South and the North.

(14) The trading of products of daily necessity for the convenience of residents of both sides.

(15) The joint development and utilization of natural resources between the South and the North to enhance the national economy.

(16) The exchange of technicians and exhibitions of manufactured products to contribute to the industrial development of the South and the North.

(17) The creation of sports facilities inside the Demilitarized Zone for goodwill matches between the South and the North.

(18) The conducting of a joint academic survey to study the ecological system of the fauna and flora inside the Demilitarized Zone.

(19) The complete removal of military facilities from within the Demilitarized Zone in order to alleviate military tension between the South and the North.

(20) The discussion of measures to control arms between the South and the North, and the installing and operation of a direct telephone line between the officials responsible for the military affairs of the two sides.

## REFERENCE

Korea, Republic of, National Unification Board. (1982). "Proposal of Minister of National Unification for Practical Pilot Projects," *South-North Dialogue in Korea*, 28 (March): 70–72.

# Select Bibliography

Ambio. (1983). "Environmental Research and Management Priorities for the 1980's," *Ambio: A Journal of the Human Environment*, 12 (2), entire issue.

Amnesty International. (1979). *The Death Penalty*. London: Amnesty International.

———. (1987). *Amnesty International, 1987, Report*. London: Amnesty International.

Arterton, F. Christopher. (1987). *Teledemocracy*. Beverly Hills, CA: Sage.

Auerbach, Gerald. (1983). *Justice Without Law?* New York: Oxford University Press.

Axelrod, Robert. (1970). *Conflict of Interest*. Chicago: Markham.

Barber, Benjamin. (1985). *Strong Democracy*. Berkeley: University of California Press.

Barnet, Richard J., and Muller, Ronald E. (1974). *Global Reach*. New York: Simon & Schuster.

Barrera, Mario, and Haas, Ernst B. (1969). "The Operationalization of Some Variables Related to Regional Integration: A Research Note," *International Organization*, 23 (October): 150–60.

Barry, Brian, and Hardin, Russell, eds. (1982). *Rational Man and Irrational Society?* Beverly Hills, CA: Sage.

Becker, Ted. (1986). "Paradox in the New American Mediation Movement: Status Quo and Social Transformation," *Missouri Journal of Dispute Resolution*: 109–29.

———. (1987). *Mediating the Nuclear Stalemate*. Santa Barbara, CA: Nuclear Age Peace Foundation.

———. (1988). "Mediating and Media-ating the Nuclear Statemate." In David Krieger, ed., *Waging Peace in the Nuclear Age*. Santa Barbara, CA: Capra Publishing.

Becker, Ted, and Scarce, Richard. (1986). "Teledemocracy Emergent." In Brenda Dervin and Melvin Voigt, eds., *Progress in Communication Science*, vol. 9, pp. 263–86. Norwood, NJ: Ablex Publishing.

Becker, Ted, and Slaton, Christa Daryl. (1987). "Cross-Cultural Mediation Training," *Mediation Quarterly*, 18 (Fall): 55–66.

Bell, Coral. (1971). *The Conventions of Crisis*. London: Oxford University Press.

Bercovitch, Jacob. (1984). *Social Conflicts and Third Parties: Strategies of Conflict Resolution*. Boulder, CO: Westview.

Black, Cyril E., et al. (1968). *Neutralization and World Politics*. Princeton, NJ: Princeton University Press.

Buchanan, James M. (1975). *The Limits of Liberty*. Chicago: University of Chicago Press.

Burton, John. (1969). *Conflict and Communication*. London: Macmillan.

———. (1975). "Alternatives to Confrontation: North-South Korean Relations," *Korean Journal of International Studies*, 6 (1): 11–16.

———. (1979). *Deviance, Terrorism, and War*. New York: St. Martin's.

———. (1984). *Global Conflict: The Domestic Sources of International Conflict*. College Park, MD: Center for International Development.

———. (1987). *Resolving Deep-Rooted Conflict: A Handbook*. Lanham, MD: University Press of America.

Carnevale, P., and Pegnetter, R. (1985). "The Selection of Mediation Tactics in Public Sector Disputes," *Journal of Social Issues*, 41 (2): 65–81.

Chosen Sotokufu. (1930). *Chosen kyosan shugi undo jiken hanketsu hokokusho* [Reports on Incident of the Korean Communist Movement]. Seoul: Chosen Sotokufu.

Chun Doo-Hwan. (1982). *New Year Policy Statement*. Seoul: Republic of Korea.

Chung, Dae-Haw. (1980). *Toward a Pluralistic Security Community: The Relevance of Integration Theory for Divided Nations with Special Emphasis on the Case of Korea*. Philadelphia: unpublished Ph.D. diss., University of Pennsylvania.

Clough, Ralph N. (1978). "Internal Trends in the Two Koreas," paper presented at the Woodrow Wilson International Center for Scholars, April 6.

Cooper, Richard N. (1968). *The Economics of Interdependence*. New York: McGraw-Hill.

Dator, James A. (1981). "Inventing a Judiciary for the State of Ponape," *Political Science*, 33 (June): 94–99.

Dennis, Peter, and Preston, Adrian, eds. (1976). *Soldiers as Statesmen*. New York: Barnes & Noble.

Deutsch, Karl W. (1953). *Nationalism and Social Communication*. New York: Wiley.

———. (1954). *Political Community at the International Level*. Garden City, NY: Doubleday.

Deutsch, Karl W., and Foltz, William J., eds. (1963). *Nation Building*. New York: Atherton.

Deutsch, Karl W., et al. (1957). *Political Community and the North Atlantic Area*. Princeton, NJ: Princeton University Press.

Dryzek, John S., and Hunter, Susan. (1987). "Environmental Mediation for

International Problems," *International Studies Quarterly*, 31 (1): 87–102.

Eisenhower, Dwight David. (1961). "Farewell Broadcast, January 7, 1961," *The Spoken Word* (SW–9403) [sound recording].

Ellsburg, Daniel. (1975). "The Theory and Practice of Nuclear Blackmail." In Oran R. Young, ed., *Bargaining*, pp. 343–63. Urbana, IL: University of Illinois Press.

Etzioni, Amitai. (1965). *Political Unification*. New York: Holt, Rinehart and Winston.

Felstiner, W. L. F., and Williams, Lynne A. (1978). "Mediation as an Alternative to Criminal Prosecution: Ideology and Limitations," *Law and Human Behavior*, 2 (3): 223–44.

Ferguson, Marilyn. (1981). *The Aquarian Conspiracy*. Los Angeles: Tarcher.

Fisher, Roger. (1969). *International Conflict for Beginners*. New York: Harper & Row.

Frank, Jerome. (1949). *Courts on Trial*. Princeton: Princeton University Press.

Frohlich, Norman, and Oppenheimer, Joe A. (1978). *Modern Political Economy*. Englewood Cliffs, NJ: Prentice-Hall.

Galtung, Johan. (1972). "Divided Nations as a Process: The Case of Korea," *Journal of Peace Research*, 9 (4): 345–60.

———. (1978). *Peace and Social Structure, Essays in Peace Research*, vol. 3. Copenhagen: Ejlers.

———. (1980). *Peace Problems: Some Case Studies, Essays in Peace Research*, vol. 5. Copenhagen: Ejlers.

———. (n.d.-a). "Alternative Life Styles in Rich Countries," *Papers* (No. 29), Chair in Conflict and Peace Research, University of Oslo.

———. (n.d.-b). "China After Mao," *Papers* (No. 61), Chair in Conflict and Peace Research, University of Oslo.

———. (n.d.-c). "Social Imperialism and Sub-Imperialism," *Papers* (No. 22), Chair in Conflict and Peace Research, University of Oslo.

———. (n.d.-d). "Alternative Life Styles in Rich Countries," *Papers* (No. 29), Chair in Conflict and Peace Research, University of Oslo.

Galtung, Johan, and Lodgaard, Sverre, eds. (1970). *Cooperation in Europe*. Oslo: University of Oslo.

Galtung, Johan, and Nishimura, Fumiko. (1974). *Learning from the Chinese People*. Oslo: University of Oslo.

George, Alexander L., Hall, David K., and Simons, William R. (1971). *The Limits of Coercive Diplomacy*. Boston: Little, Brown.

Gorbachev, Mikhail. (1987). *Perestroika*. New York: Harper & Row.

Gross, John. (1969). *The Economics of Bargaining*. New York: Basic Books.

Haas, Ernst B. (1958). *The Uniting of Europe*. Stanford, CA: Stanford University Press.

———. (1964). *Beyond the Nation State*. Stanford, CA: Stanford University Press.

———. (1966). "International Intergration: The European and the Universal Process." In Amitai Etzioni, ed., *International Political Communities*, pp. 93–129. Garden City, NY: Doubleday.

Haas, Ernst B., and Schmitter, Phillipe C. (1966). "Economics and Differential

Patterns of Political Integration: Projections About Unity in Latin America." In Amitai Etzioni, ed., *International Political Communities*, pp. 259–99. Garden City, NY: Doubleday.

Haas, Michael. (1974). *International Systems*. San Francisco: Chandler.

———. (1984). "Paradigms of Political Integration and Unification: Applications to Korea," *Journal of Conflict Resolution*, 21 (1): 47–60.

———. (1985). *Basic Data of Asian Regional Organizations*. Volume 9 of *Basic Documents of Asian Regional Organizations*. Dobbs Ferry, NY: Oceana Publications.

———. (in preparation). *The Asian Way to Peace: A Story of Regional Cooperation*. New York: Praeger Publishers.

Hansen, Roger D. (1969). "Regional Integration: Reflections on a Decade of Theoretical Efforts," *World Politics*, 21 (January): 242–71.

Hardin, Russell. (1982). *Collective Action*. Baltimore: Johns Hopkins Press.

Harrison, Selig. (1987). "The 'Great Follower': Kim Il Sung Promotes a Chinese-Style Open-Door Policy," *Far Eastern Economic Review*, 138 (December 2): 36–38.

Hayek, Friedrich A. (1973). *Rules and Order*. Chicago: University of Chicago Press.

Henderson, Gregory. (1987). "Time to Change the US-South Korea Military Relationship," *Far Eastern Economic Review*, 138 (October 22): 40.

Holshek, C. J. (1982). *The Military and Strategic Balance: East Asia and the Pacific*. Washington, DC: Woodrow Wilson Center.

Humana, Charles. (1987). *World Human Rights Guide*. London: Pan.

International Foundation for Development Alternatives. (1981). "Manifesto of Nobel Prize Winners," *IFDA Dossier* (September-October): 1(61)–3(63).

Janis, Irving L. (1972). *Victims of Groupthink*. Boston: Houghton Mifflin.

Kang, Young Hoon. (1987). "Diplomatic Aspects of Korean Unification." Paper presented at the International Conference on Korean Unification Problem Revisited, Seoul, August 20–21.

Keohane, Robert O., and Nye, Joseph S. (1977). *Power and Interdependence*. Boston: Little, Brown.

Keyes, Gene. (1982). "Force Without Firepower: A Doctrine of Unarmed Military Service," *CoEvolution Quarterly*, 34 (Summer): 4–25.

Kidron, Michael, and Segal, Ronald. (1981). *The State of the World Atlas*. New York: Simon & Schuster.

Kim Chong-Bom and Kim Tong-Un. (1945). *Haebang chonhu ui Choson chinsang* [Korea Before and After the Liberation]. Seoul: Choson chon'gyong yon'guhoe.

Kim Hak-Chun. (1983). *Han'guk chongch'iron: Yon'gu ui hyonhwanggwa panghyang* [Korean Politics: The Present, Status and Direction of Research]. Seoul: Han'gilsa.

Kim Il Sung. (1969). *Namchoson hyongmyong kaw choguk t'ongil e taehayo* [On South Korean Revolution and National Reunification]. Pyongyang: Choson nodongdang ch'ulp'ansa.

———. (1976). *Chojak sonjip* [Selected Works]. Pyongyang: Choson nondongdang ch'ulp'ansa.

————. (1980). "Report to the Sixth Congress of the Workers' Party of Korea on the Work of the Central Committee," *Korea Today*, 11, 290: 14–68.

Kim, Jin-Hyun. (1987). "Economic Aspects of Korea Unification," paper presented at the International Conference on Korean Unification Problem Revisited, Seoul, August 20–21.

Koenig, Louis W. (1971). *Bryan*. New York: Putnam's Sons.

Koh, Young Bok. (1987). "Social-Cultural Aspects of Korean Unification," paper presented at the International Conference on Korean Unification Problem Revisited, Seoul, August 20–21.

Korea, Republic of, National Unification Board. (1982). "Proposal of Minister of National Unification for Practical Pilot Projects," *South-North Dialogue in Korea*, 28 (March): 70–72.

Korea, Republic of. (1984). *Inter-Korean Economic Talks: A Sign of Thaw?* Seoul: Korean Overseas Information Service.

————. (1986a). *A Bibliographic Catalogue of English Publications*. Seoul: National Unification Board.

————. (1986b). *A Comparative Study of the South and North Korean Economies*. Seoul: National Unification Board.

————. (1987). *New Initiatives for Peace in Korea*. Seoul: Korean Overseas Information Service.

Kuhn, Thomas S. (1970). *The Structure of Scientific Revolutions*, 2nd ed. Chicago: University of Chicago Press.

Levy, Marion J., Jr. (1972). *Modernization: Latecomers and Survivors*. New York: Basic Books.

Lindberg, Leon N., and Scheingold, Stuart A., eds. (1971). *Regional Integration: Theory and Research*. Cambridge, MA: Harvard University Press.

Luce, R. Duncan, and Raiffa, Howard. (1957). *Games and Decisions*. New York: Wiley.

March, James G., and Simon, Herbert A. (1958). *Organizations*. New York: Wiley.

Mazzini, Giuseppe. (1907). *The Duties of Man and Other Essays*. London: Dent.

McCormack, Gavan. (1978). "Reunification: Problems and Prospects." In Gavan McCormack and Mark Selden, eds., *Korea, North and South*, Ch. 12. New York: Monthly Review Press.

McGillis, Daniel, and Mullen, Joan. (1977). *Neighborhood Justice Centers*. Washington, DC: U.S. Department of Justice.

Mendlovitz, Saul H., ed. (1975). *On the Creation of a Just Order*. New York: Free Press.

Mitrany, David. (1966). *A Working Peace System*. Chicago: Quadrangle.

Osgood, Charles E. (1962). *An Alternative to War or Surrender*. Urbana: University of Illinois Press.

Paige, Glenn D. (1965). "Some Implications for Political Science of the Comparative Politics of Korea," *International Conference on the Problems of Modernization in Asia (June 28–July 7, 1965) Report*. Seoul: Korea University, Asiatic Research Center: 388–405. Reprinted in Fred Riggs, ed., *Frontiers of Development Administration*, pp. 139–70. Durham, NC: Duke University Press, 1970.

————. (1980). "Nonviolent Political Science," *Social Alternatives* (Brisbane), 1 (June): 104–12.

————. (1984). "Nonviolent Cultural Resources for Korean Reunification." In Sung-Joo Han, ed., *Korea and Asia*, pp. 227–50. Seoul: Korea University Press. Essay written in honor of the sixtieth birthday of Professor Kim Jun-Yop.

————. (1985). "Transnational Consortium for Study of Korean Reunification: A Nonviolent Proposal," paper prepared for the International Symposium on the Reunification of Korea and Peace in Asia, sponsored by the Asian-Pacific Peace Policy Institute, Yokohama International Hall, Japan, July 6–8.

Pennock, J. Roland, and Chapman, John W., eds. (1972). *Coercion.* New York: Atherton. (Vol. 14 of *Nomos*.)

Plimak, E. G., and Karyakin, Yu. F. (1979). "Lenin o mirnoi i nemirnoi formakh revolyutsionnogo perekhoda v sotsializmu" [Lenin on Peaceful and Nonpeaceful Forms of Revolutionary Transition to Socialism], paper presented at the eleventh World Congress of the International Political Science Association, Moscow, August 12–18.

Puchala, Donald. (1981). "Integration Theory and the Study of International Relations." In Richard L. Merritt and Karl W. Deutsch, eds., *From National Development to Global Community*, ch. 6. London: Allen & Unwin.

Pye, Lucien W., and Verba, Sidney, eds. (1965). *Political Culture and Political Development.* Princeton, NJ: Princeton University Press.

Rapoport, Anatol. (1960). *Fights, Games, and Debates.* Ann Arbor: University of Michigan Press.

————. (1964). *Strategy and Conscience.* New York: Schocken.

————. (1966a). "Strategic and Non-Strategic Approaches to Problems of Security and Peace." In Kathleen Archibald, ed., *Strategic Interaction and Conflict.* Berkeley: University of California Press.

————. (1966b). *Two-Person Game Theory.* Ann Arbor: University of Michigan Press.

Research Center for Peace and Unification. (1978). *Korea's Quest for Peaceful Unification: Its History and Prospects for the Future.* Seoul: Research Center for Peace and Unification.

Roehl, J. A., and Cook, R. (1985). "Issues in Mediation: Rhetoric and Reality Revisited," *Journal of Social Issues*, 41 (2): 161–78.

Rokeach, Milton. (1960). *The Open and the Cold Mind.* New York: Basic Books.

Rummel, R. J. (1984). *In the Minds of Men: Principles Toward Understanding and Waging Peace.* Seoul: Sogang University Press.

————. (1987). "American Troops in Korea and the Potential for War," unpublished manuscript.

Sakamoto, Yoshikazu. (1978). *Korea as a World Order Issue.* New York: Institute for World Order.

Satin, Mark. (1979). *New Age Politics.* New York: Dell.

Scalapino, Robert A. (1976). "The Two Koreas—Dialogue or Conflict?" In William J. Barnds, ed. *The Two Koreas in East Asian Affairs*, pp. 60–112. New York: New York University Press.

Schelling, Thomas C. (1960). *The Strategy of Conflict*. Cambridge, MA: Harvard University Press.

———. (1966). *Arms and Influence*. New Haven, CT: Yale University Press.

Schelling, Thomas C., and Halperin, Morton. (1961). *Strategy and Arms Control*. New York: Twentieth Century Fund.

Schubert, James N. (1978). "Toward a 'Working Peace System' in Asia: Organizational Growth and State Participation in Asian Regionalism," *International Organization*, 22 (Spring): 425–62.

Sharp, Gene. (1973). *The Politics of Nonviolent Action*. Boston: Porter Sargent.

Shonholtz, Raymond. (1984). "Neighborhood Justice Systems: Work, Structure, and Guiding Principles," *Mediation Quarterly*, 15 (September): 1–24.

Snieder, Richard L. (1979). "Prospects for Korean Security." In *Asian Security in the 1980's*, pp. 7–20. Washington, DC: Office of the Assistant Secretary of Defense for International Security Affairs.

Snyder, Glenn H. (1972). "Crisis Bargaining." In Charles F. Hermann, ed., *International Crises*, pp. 217–56. New York: Free Press.

Thoennis, N. A., and Pearson, J. (1985). "Predicting Outcomes in Divorce Mediation: The Influence of People and Process," *Journal of Social Issues*, 41 (2): 115–26.

Toffler, Alvin. (1980). *The Third Wave*. New York: Bantam.

United Nations, General Assembly. (1948). *Universal Declaration of Human Rights*. New York: United Nations. Adopted December 10, 1948.

———. (1978). *Final Document of Assembly Session on Disarmament, 23 May–1 July 1978* (S–10/2). New York: UN Office of Public Information.

———. (1982). *World Charter for Nature* (Resolution 37/7). New York: United Nations. Adopted October 28, 1982.

United States, Department of State, Arms Control and Disarmament Agency. (1987). *World Military Expenditures and Arms Transfers, 1986*. Washington, DC: Government Printing Office.

Vincent, Jack. (1987). "On Rummel's Omnipresent Theory," *International Studies Quarterly*, 31 (1): 119–25.

Walton, Richard E., and McKersie, Robert B. (1965). *A Behavioral Theory of Labor Negotiations*. New York: McGraw-Hill.

Warhaftig, Paul. (1984). "Nonprofessional Conflict Resolution," *Villanova Law Review*, 29 (6): 1,463–474.

White, Nathan. (1978). "The Necessity for a German Solution to the Korean Problem," *Korea and World Affairs*, 2 (Fall): 349–68.

White, Ralph K. (1968). *Nobody Wanted War*. Garden City, NY: Doubleday.

Yang, Sung Chul. (1987). "Korean Reunification: A Comparative Perspective," paper prepared for presentation at the International Conference on Korean Unification Problem Revisited, Seoul, August 20–21.

Young, Oran R. (1968). *The Politics of Force*. Princeton, NJ: Princeton University Press.

———. (1969). "Interdependencies and World Politics," *International Journal*, 24 (Autumn): 727–50.

Young, Oran R., ed. (1975). *Bargaining: Formal Theories of Negotiation*. Urbana, IL: University of Illinois Press.

Yu, Suk-Ryul. (1986). "Unification Strategies of South and North Korea," *Korea & World Affairs*, 10 (Winter): 776–97.

Zhang Yiping. (1982). "Due feibaoli zhuyi ying jiben kending" [We Should Positively Affirm Nonviolence], *Shijie lishi* [World History], 16 (June 7): 78–80.

# Index

Algeria, 19

Ambio, 56

Anti-Communist Laws (1981 revision), 86

"Aquarian Conspiracy," 75

Armenians, as divided people, 35

Armistice Agreement at Panmunjom, 2–3

arms freeze, as step in Korean reunification, 110

Arterton, F. Christopher, 84

Asian African Legal Consultative Committee, 43

Asian Games (1986), 8

"Asian Way," in negotiation, 37

Association of South East Asian Nations (ASEAN), 45

Auerbach, Gerald, 76

Austro-Hungarian empire, unification of, 93

Barber, Benjamin, 83–84

bargaining: coercive diplomacy and, 99–100; distributive bargaining, 95–98; payoff space in negotiations, 95–98

Barrera, Mario, 37

Barry, Brian, 105

basic needs satisfaction, in socialism, 18

Becker, Ted, 75, 76, 85; third-track conflict resolution, 83–84

Bercovitch, Jacob, 81

biosphere, Korean reunification and, 62

Bulgaria, 27

Burma, 36

Burton, John, 56, 103; second-track diplomacy, 81

Camp David Accords, 69

capitalism: cooperation with socialist systems, 17–19; economic relations with socialist countries, 19–26; joint ventures and, 22; political relations with socialist countries, 26–32

Carnevale, P., 80

Carter, Jimmy, 6–7; Camp David Accords and, 69

Central Intelligence Agency (Korean), 5

change of generations. See T + 40 years

China. See People's Republic of China

Chun Doo-Hwan, 7, 8, 10, 42
Churchill, Winston, 36
citizen mediation, 76
Clough, Ralph N., 108, 110
coercive diplomacy, Korean reunification and, 99–102
Combined Armed Forces Command Agreement, 6–7
communication, mediation programs and, 77
conflict resolution: interpersonal mediation movement, 76–79; and Korean reunification, 76–84; third party international conflict resolution (TPICR), 81–84; third-track conflict resolution, 83–84, 84–87
Cook, R., 77
Costa Rica, in third-track conflict resolution, 84
Council for Mutual Economic Assistance (COMECON), 61
Cuba, 19, 28, 31; U.S. blockade, 25
Cyprus, divided peoples in, 35

Dante, 36
Dator, James A., 78
Demilitarized Zone (DMZ), 3, 4, 6, 39, 45–48
Democratic Confederal Republic of Koryo (DCRK), 6, 15, 33, 60–63, 109; ten-point proposal for, 131–132
Democratic Front for the reunification of the Fatherland, 2, 4
Democratic People's Republic of Korea (DPRK). *See* North Korea
democratization, of Korea, 118–20
Deng Xiaoping, 73
detente: theory of, 44–45; U.S.-Soviet, 111
Deutsch, Karl, 37–38, 92
Die Grünen, 64
Directors General of Civil Aviation, 43–44
disarmament, 60–61
distributive bargaining, 95–98
divided peoples, in international affairs, 35–36

DMZ. *See* Demilitarized Zone
DPRK. *See* North Korea
Dryzek, John S., 80

ECDC (Economic Cooperation among Developing Countries), 38
Economic Cooperation among Developing Countries (ECDC), 38
economic development, and Korean reunification, 120–22
economic well-being: Korean demilitarization and, 61; North-South comparison of gross national product, 121
economics, capitalism versus socialism, 17–26
Edgeworth box diagram, 95–96
Egypt: Camp David Accords, 69; Korean promise, 32; Sadat visit to Israel, 44
Eisenhower, Dwight D., and revolution of peace, 53–54
electronic town meetings (ETMs), 83–84
environment, biosphere preservation and Korean reunification, 62
Etzioni, Amitai, 37
European Economic Community (EEC), 61

Felstiner, W. L. F., 77
Ferguson, Marilyn, 75
Fiji, 36
Finland, 16
foreign trade, in capitalism, 18
France, 92
functionalism, definition of, 106
Functionalist approach: Korean reunification, 35–50; theories of, 36–38

Galtung, Johan, 40
Gandhi Rural University, 64
George, Alexander L., 101
Germany, 24; change of generations, 13–15; divided peoples in, 35
*glasnost*, 73

Gorbachev, Mikhail, 28, 47; *peres-troika* and *glasnost*, 72–73
Great National Congress, 6
Greece, 27
Gross, John, 97
gross national product: definition of, 18; North-South comparision, 121, 124

Haas, Ernst, 37
Hall, David K., 101
Hansen, Roger, 37
Hardin, Russell, 105
Harrison, Selig, 10
Hayek, Friedrich A., 105
Henderson, Gregory, 3, 39
holocaust, "silent holocaust," 55
human rights, Korean reunification and, 61–62
Hungary, 15
Hunter, Susan, 80

India, 27, 36; Shanti Sena (Peace Brigade), 64; Soviet Union and, 25–26
INF treaty, 75
integration, theories of, 36–38
international diplomacy, and Korean reunification, 79–84
International Olympic Committee (IOC), 1, 84, 126
international relations theory: detente theory, 44–45; and Korean unification, 1–2
Interparliamentary Union (IPU), 6
interpersonal mediation movement, and conflict resolution, 76–79
IPU (Interparliamentary Union), 6
Ireland, 84; divided peoples in, 35
Israel: Camp David Accords, 69; Sadat visit, 44

Janis, Irving, 104
Japan, 43, 58; anti-Japanese sentiments in Korea, 122; diplomatic relations normalized with, 120
Joint Communique of 1972, 4, 5
joint venture, definition of, 22

joint ventures, as step in Korean reunification, 110

Kang, Young Hoon, 43
Kant, Immanuel, 36
Karyakin, Yu, 65
Keyes, Gene, 55
Kim Dae-Jung, 4, 5, 7, 8, 10, 32
Kim Il Sung, 2–4, 9, 42, 117, 119, 122–26
Kim Jong Il, 120, 123–24
Kim Jong Pil, 39
Kim Young-Sam, 10
Koh Young Bok, 47
Korea: anti-Japanese sentiments, 122; Armistice Agreement at Panmunjom, 2–3; Armistice Agreement with U.S., 2–3; Association of South East Asian Nations (ASEAN) and, 45–46; capitalist versus socialist economics, 19–26; capitalist versus socialist ideologies, 17–19; Central Intelligence Agency (Korean), 5; Council for Mutual Economic Assistance (COMECON) and, 61; creative problem-solving potential, 57–60; danger of North-South division, 69–72; Demilitarzed Zone (DMZ), 3, 4, 6, 36, 45–48; democratizing of, 118–20; demographics, 91–92; Directors General of Civil Aviation meeting, 43–44; disarmament, 60–61; divided peoples in, 35; economic development, 120–22; European Economic Community (EEC) and, 61; external political developments, 72–75; global leadership potential, 58–60; Korean War, 2–4; Kwangju massacre, 7, 58; Military Armistice Commission (MAC), 2–3, 40, 48; military reductions, 124–26; North-South conflict background, 1–3; North-South economic relations, 19–26; North-South Joint Communique of 1972, 4; North-South political relations and, 26–

33; North-South rapprochement efforts, 4–11; Olympic Games of 1988, 1, 8, 10–12, 43, 48, 70, 111, 126–28; peace treaty with U.S., 6–7; People's Republic of China political changes and, 73–74; pilot projects for facilitation of Korean reunification, 133–34; pluralistic ideological orientation, 122–24; postwar developments and North-South split, 91–93; Reagan's Korean aid policy, 40–41; revolution of peace, 53–56; South Korean Red Cross, 4, 5, 39, 48, 84; Soviet Union political changes and, 72–73; Strategic Talks for Arms Reduction (START), 9; U.S. transformationalism and, 74–75; U.S.-North Korean peace treaty, 8–9; U.S.-Soviet cold war, 72. *See also* Korean reunification; North Korea; South Korea

Korea Military Armistice Commission, 48

Korean Air 858 explosion, 11–12, 58

Korean reunification: Anti-Communist Laws (1981 revision), 86, 123; attitudinal factors, 38–40; biosphere preservation, 62; coercive diplomacy, 99–102; conflict resolution approaches, 76–84; creative problem-solving potential and, 57–60; cultural arenas for interaction, 47–48; Democratic Confederal Republic of Korea plan, 7–8; democratizing Korea, 118–20; dependent variable of peaceful unification, 92–94; disarmament and, 60–61; distributive bargaining, 95–98; economic arenas for interaction, 45–47; economic development and, 120–22; economic well-being and, 61; favorable conditions for, 84–86; functionalist approach, 35–50; future possibilities, 108–12; global resources, 63–66; history of, 1–12; human rights and, 61–62; international diplomacy, 79–84; international relations theory and, 1–2; interpersonal mediation movement lessons, 76–79; lessons from other countries, 14–16; mediation approach, 69–88; military reductions, 124–26; negotiated unification, 94–98; negotiation approach, 10, 91–112; neutralization approach, 13–29; nonviolence approach, 53–66; nonviolent global transformation and, 60–65; North-South economic relations and, 19–26; North-South political relations and, 26–33; North-South rapprochement efforts, 4–11; payoff space in negotiations, 95–98; peaceful problem-solving processes, 62–63; pilot projects for facilitation of, 133–34; pluralistic ideological orientation effects on, 122–24; political arenas for interaction, 40–45; political feasibility of, 117–28; possibilities of peaceful cooperation, 17–19, 32–33; problem-solving strategies, 102–5; problems identified, 86–87; Red Cross meetings, 4–5, 39, 48, 84; and revolution of peace, 53–56; seeking commonality and, 126–28; social arenas for interaction, 47–48; spontaneous unification, 105–7; T + 40 principle, 13–17, 32; tasks for global transformation, 54–56; ten-point proposal for Democratic Republic of Koryo, 131–32; theories of, 36–38; U.S.-Soviet cold war and, 72; UN Commission for Unification and Reconstruction of Korea (UNCURK), 2. *See also* Korea; North Korea; South Korea

Korean War: after effects, 117–18; beginning, 2–3; Soviet Union and, 2

Koryo. *See* Democratic Confederal Republic of Koryo (DCRK)

Kunsan Air Base, 3

Kurds, as divided people, 35

Kwangju massacre, 7, 58

Li Gun-Mo, 10
Lindberg, Leon N., 106
Lucas Aerospace Limited, 64
Luce, R. Duncan, 95, 96

MAC. *See* Military Armistice Commission
MacArthur, Douglas, 2
McGillis, Daniel, 76
McKersie, Robert B., 98
Malaysian Sabah, 36
Malvinas Islands, 36
Mao Zedong, 22–23, 64
Mazzini, Giuseppi, 35–36
mediation approach: citizen mediation, 76; conflict resolution, 76–84; international diplomacy and, 79–84; second-track diplomacy, 81; third party international conflict resolution (TPICR), 81–84; third-track conflict resolution, 83–84; to Korean reunification, 69–88
Military Armistice Commission (MAC), 2–3, 40, 48
military reductions, and Korean reunification, 124–26
Mitrany, David, 37
Moros, as divided people, 35
Moscow Conference of 1945, 2
Movimiento (Spain), 30
Mullen, Joan, 76

negotiation approach: "Asian Way," 37; coercive diplomacy, 99–102; dependent variable of peaceful unification, 92–94; distributive bargaining, 95–98; Edgeworth box diagram, 95–96; negotiated unification, 94–98; payoff space in negotiations, 95–98; problem-solving strategies, 102–5; spontaneous unification, 105–7; to Korean reunification, 91–112
neofunctionalism, definition of, 106
Neutral Nations Supervisory Commission, 9
neutralization approach, to Korean reunification, 13–29

New Caledonia, 36
New International Economic Order (NIEO), 37–38
New Zealand, in third-track conflict resolution, 84
Nicaragua, 19
NIEO (New International Economic Order), 37–38
Nixon Doctrine, 3
nonviolence approach: disarmament and, 60–61; global resources and, 63–66; Korea's creative problem-solving potential and, 57–60; nonviolent global transformation and, 60–65; peaceful unification factors, 93–94; revolution of peace, 53–56; tasks for global transformation, 54–56; to Korean reunification, 53–66
North Korea: armed forces strength, 124; attitudes toward South Korea, 38–40; coercive diplomacy of, 100–102; danger of division, 69–72; demilitarization talks, 40–43; Democratic Confederal Republic of Korea plan, 7–8; Directors General of Civil Aviation meeting, 43–44; distributive bargaining and payoff space, 95–98; economic relations with South, 19–26; free trade issues, 47; government of, 2; Kim Il Sung's policy, 117–18; Kim Il Sung's reign, 118–21; Korean War, 2–4; negotiated unification, 94–99; North-South Joint Communique of 1972, 4, 5; Olympic Games of 1988; 1, 8, 10–12; political relations with South, 26–33; postwar developments, 91; rapprochement efforts, 4–11; U.S. peace treaty, 6–7; U.S.-North Korean peace treaty, 8–9. *See also* Korea; Korean reunification
North-South Joint Communique of 1972, 4, 5
North-South Joint Coordinating Committee, 5
Northern Ireland, 84

Olympic Games of 1988, 1, 8, 10–12, 43, 48, 70, 111, 126–28
Organization of Petroleum Exporting Countries (OPEC), 37–38
Osgood, Charles, 40

Pacific Science Association, 48
pacifism. *See* nonviolence approach
Paige, Glenn D., 65
Palestinians, as divided people, 35
Park, 126
Park Chung Hee, 4–6, 121; assassination of, 7
payoff space, and distributive bargaining, 95–98
Pearson, J., 79
Pegnetter, R., 80
People's Democracy of Korea, 70
People's Republic of China, 4, 6; divided peoples in, 35; economic policies, 22–23, 25; environmental policy support for Korea, 62; Liberation Army, 31; political changes in, 73–74; post-Maoist, 73–74; Taiwan relations, 87; in third-track conflict resolution, 84
*perestroika*, 72–73
Philippine Mindanao, 35–36
Philippines, 74
Plimak, E. G., 65
pluralistic ideological orientation, and Korean reunification, 122–24
Poland, solidarity movement in, 64
propaganda, as step in Korean reunification, 110

Raiffa, Howard, 95, 96
Rangoon bomb assassinations, 58
Rapoport, Anatol, 94, 102, 105
Reagan, Ronald: Korean aid policy, 40–41; U.S. transformationalism and, 74–75
recognition, as step in Korean reunification, 110
Red Cross, 4, 5, 39, 48, 84
Republic of Korea (ROK). *See* South Korea
Revolution of peace, 53–56

Rhee, Syngman, 2, 119, 122, 125
Roehl, J. A., 77
Rogers, Felix, 4
Rogers, William, 4
Roh Tae-Woo, 10
Rokeach, Milton, 103
Royal Swedish Academy of Sciences, 56
Rummel, R. J., 71
Rusk, Dean, 31

Sadat, Anwar, visit to Israel, 44
Samoa, divided peoples in, 35
Scalapino, Robert A., 104
Scarce, Richard, 83–84
Scheingold, Stuart A., 106
Schelling, 101
Schelling, Thomas C., 96, 99
Schmitter, Philippe C., 37
Schubert, James, 37
self-reliance, in capitalism and socialism, 18
Shanti Sena (Peace Brigade), 64
Sharp, Gene, 65
Shonholtz, Raymond, 77
"silent holocaust," 55
Simons, William R., 101
Slaton, Christa Daryl, 85
Sneider, Richard L., 110
Snyder, Glenn H., 101
socialism: cooperation with capitalist systems, 17–19; economic relations with capitalist countries, 19–26; joint ventures and, 22; political relations with capitalist countries, 26–32
Solidarity (Poland), 64
South Korea: Anti-Communist Laws (1981 revision), 86; anti-communist laws, 123; armed forces strength, 124; attitudes toward North Korea, 38–40; as bridgehead for capitalism, 29; coercive diplomacy, 100–102; danger of division, 69–72; demilitarization talks, 40–43; diplomatic relations normalized with Japan, 102; Directors General of Civil Aviation

meeting, 43–44; distributive bargaining and payoff space, 95–98; economic relations with North, 19–26; government of, 2; Korean War, 2–4; Kwangju massacre, 7; negotiated unification, 94–99; North-South Joint Communique of 1972, 4, 5; Park assassination, 7; political relations with North, 26–33; postwar developments, 91; rapprochement efforts, 4–11; South Korean Red Cross, 4, 5; U.S. peace treaty, 6–7. *See also* Korea; Korean reunification

South Korean Red Cross, 4
South-North Economic Cooperation Committee, 45
Soviet Union, 19, 23–24; authoritarian rule in Soviet system, 28–31; cold war, 72; detente, 111; environmental policy support for Korea, 62; India and, 25–26; in Korean War, 2; People's Republic of China political changes and, 73–74; political changes in, 72–73; Strategic Talks for Arms Reduction (START), 9; in third-track conflict resolution, 84; U.S. transformationalism and, 74–75
Spain: change of generations, 14; compared to Yugoslavia, 29–30
spontaneous unification, conditions for, 105–7
Sri Lanka, 36, 84
Strategic Talks for Arms Reduction (START), 9
Sulu archipelago, 36
Sulu Sultanate, 35
Sung. *See* Kim Il Sung
Sweden, 16; in third-track conflict resolution, 84
Switzerland, 15; in third-track conflict resolution, 84

T + 40 principle, 13—17, 32
Taiwan, relations with People's Republic of China, 87

Terrorism, Korean Air 858 explosion, 11–12
third party international conflict resolution (TPICR), 81–84
Third World, 22–26; contrasted with First and Second, 65; definition of, 24–25; New International Economic Order, 37–38
third-track conflict resolution, 84–87
Thoennis, N. A., 79
Toffler, Alvin, 75
transaction flows, definition of, 36
Transformational movement, 74–75
trauma. *See* T + 40 years

UNC. *See* United Nations Command
UNCTAD (United Nations Conference on Trade and Development), 6
UNCURK. *See* United Nations Commission for Unification and Reconstruction of Korea
unification: coercive diplomacy and, 99–102; functionalism and neofunctionalism, 106; negotiated, 94–99; peaceful, 93–94; political conditions affecting, 92–93; preconditions for, 36–37; theories of, 35–38; transaction flows defined, 36. *See also* Korean reunification
United Farm Workers Union, 64
United Nations, Association of South East Asian Nations (ASEAN) and, 45–46
United Nations Command (UNC), 2–4, 6, 40
United Nations Commission for Unification and Reconstruction of Korea (UNCURK), 2, 6
United Nations Conference on Trade and Development (UNCTAD), 6
United Nations General Assembly Special Sessions on Disarmament (1978), 60–61
United Nations World Charter for Nature, 56
United States: Armistice Agreement at Panmunjom, 2–3; Camp David

Accords, 69; cold war, 72; Cuban blockade, 25; demilitarization talks with Korea, 40–43; detente with Soviet Union, 40–41, 111; environmental policy support for Korea, 62; INF treaty, 75; Korean aid policy of Reagan, 40–41; Korean War, 2–4; peace treaty with Korea, 6–7; People's Republic of China political changes and, 73–74; Strategic Talks for Arms Reductions (START), 9; in third-track conflict resolution, 84; transformationalism, 74–75; troop reduction as step in Korean reunification, 111; troop reductions in Korea, 125; U.S.-North Korean peace treaty, 8–9; USA-USSR Joint Commission, 2

Vietnam, 58
Vladivostok, free port, 47

Waldheim, Kurt, 4
Walton, Richard E., 98
White, Nathan, 96
White, Ralph K., 104
Williams, Lynne A., 77
World Health Organization, 6
World Table Tennis championships, 7

Yemen, divided peoples in, 35
Yi Tonghwi, 121
Young, Oran R., 99
Yu Kuo-Hwa, 87
Yugoslavia, 16; compared to Spain, 29–30

Zhang, Yiping, 65

# About the Contributors

THEODORE L. BECKER (J.D., Rutgers; Ph.D., Northwestern) is Professor and Head of the Political Science Department at Auburn University; formerly he was with the University of Hawaii at Manoa. Author of eight books on the U.S. government and the politics of legal systems, he is presently active in developing and applying theories and methods in conflict resolution and on electronic democracy. Two books in progress are *Transformational Mediation* and *Teledemocracy Emergent*, both in cooperation with his colleague and co-author, Christa Daryl Slaton.

JOHAN GALTUNG (Reg. Mag., University of Oslo) holds joint appointments at the University of Hawaii at Manoa and the University of Witten-Herdecke. He began his career at Columbia University and has held visiting appointments at 34 institutions, most recently at Princeton, the City University of New York, and the University of California at San Diego. His publications include *The European Community* and the multivolume *Essays in Peace Research*, and his current research focuses on comparative civilization theory, development theory, and a new humanistic economics. In 1987 he won the Right Livelihood ("Alternative Nobel") Honorary Award.

MICHAEL HAAS (Ph.D., Stanford), Professor of Political Science, University of Hawaii at Manoa, is the author of *International Organization, Approaches to the Study of Political Science, International Conflict, International Systems*, and *Fundamentals of Asian Regional Cooperation*.

Currently he is preparing *The Pacific Way: Regional Cooperation in the South Pacific* (1989) and *The Asian Way to Peace: A Story of Regional Cooperation* for Praeger Publishers.

GLENN D. PAIGE (Ph.D., Northwestern), Professor of Political Science, University of Hawaii, is the author of *The Korean Decision: June 24–30, 1950* and "On Values and Science: *The Korean Decision* Reconsidered," *American Political Science Review*. At a scholarly conference in Seoul during 1968 he proposed transforming the Korean demilitarized zone (DMZ) into a Zone of Peace, including athletic facilities where events such as the Olympic Games might be held. In 1987, as a scholar of nonviolent political science, he was privileged to visit both North and South Korea.

DAE-SOOK SUH (Ph.D., Columbia), Professor of Political Science and director of the Center for Korean Studies, University of Hawaii, is the author of *The Korean Communist Movement, 1918–1948, Korean Communism, 1945–1980, Kim Il Sung,* and other works.

ORAN R. YOUNG (Ph.D., Yale) is Senior Fellow of the Dickey Endowment for International Understanding and Adjunct Professor of Government at Dartmouth College as well as Senior Fellow at the Center for Northern Studies, Wolcott, Vermont. His research centers on problems of conflict and conflict resolution and on the role of regimes or social institutions in international society. His most recent books include *International Cooperation: Building Regimes for Natural Resources and the Environment* and (with Gail Osherenko) *The Age of the Arctic: Hot Conflicts and Cold Realities*.